First published in the United States 2022 by Insight Editions
First published in Great Britain 2023 by Expanse
An imprint of HarperCollins*Publishers*
1 London Bridge Street, London SE1 9GF
www.farshore.co.uk

HarperCollins*Publishers*
Harper Ireland, Macken House, 39/40 Mayor Street Upper,
Dublin 1 D01 C9W8, Ireland

ISBN 978 0 0085 8712 3
Printed in Italy
001

A CIP catalogue record for this title is available from the British Library.

MIX
Paper | Supporting
responsible forestry
FSC™ C007454

This book is produced from independently certified FSC™ paper
to ensure responsible forest management.

For more information visit: www.harpercollins.co.uk/green

POKÉMON

COOKBOOK

Delicious Recipes Inspired by Pikachu and Friends

Victoria Rosenthal

Contents

Introduction

The world of Pokémon is a story of adventure, friendship and being the very best you can be. Although the goal is typically about forming the strongest team of Pokémon you can and defeating the reigning champion to claim the title for yourself, being the new Pokémon champion isn't possible without forming friendships and true bonds on the way. The charm of the journey is universal.

The goal of this cookbook is to take that love of Pokémon that so many people share and extend it to the wonderful world of cuisine. These recipes include all sorts of drinks, desserts and other delicious dishes that celebrate and cherish all the amazing varieties of Pokémon out there, taking inspiration from all the different types of Pokémon to think of great ways to get in the kitchen and get cooking. We can come up with Fire-type dishes that are spicy and warm you up. Electric-type dishes full of sour elements that bring a spark to your plate. Ground-type dishes that are filling and dense, and eating too much may leave you, well, grounded for a time. Each and every known type is represented in this cookbook, and I hope you enjoy the characteristics that show themselves in the meals they are tied to!

All of the recipes in this book are family friendly. Pokémon has fans of all ages, and another goal of this book is to bring the family into the kitchen and combine a love of Pokémon with a love of food. This book provides fun ways to bring those less familiar with culinary adventures into the kitchen. There are a few more complicated recipes that will require extra care and a helping hand, but there are also plenty of meals that are easily approachable for anyone new to cooking.

So let's get cooking! There are lots of fun treats and tasty dishes to enjoy. Now you can cook them all and perhaps even make some friends along the way.

Ingredients Guide

Aburaage are thinly sliced, deep-fried tofu pockets used in Japanese cuisine.

Blue spirulina is an extract from spirulina, a type of microalgae. For the recipes in this book, you will want to use the powder version of this ingredient.

Butterfly pea flowers are dried flowers that grow in Southeast Asia. The flower is dehydrated and commonly used for tea. It is used to dye things a bright blue colour.

Calabrian chilli peppers are smoky chilli peppers grown in Italy. They have a Scoville scale rating between 25,000 and 40,000 SHU.

Chinese five-spice powder is a combination of cinnamon, Szechuan peppercorns, star anise, fennel seeds and cloves. It can be stored in the pantry for up to a year, but keep in mind that spices will lose their flavour the longer they are stored.

Condensed milk is milk that has been gently heated, had 60 per cent of the water removed, been mixed with sugar and canned. This is an extremely thick, caramelised sweetened milk. It is typically found in cans that can be stored in the pantry for about a year. Once opened, it must be refrigerated and used within 2 weeks.

Evaporated milk is milk that has been gently heated and had 60 per cent of the water removed to make a dense, creamy milk. It is found in cans that can be stored in the pantry for about 6 months. Once opened, it must be refrigerated and used within 5 days.

Gochujang is a Korean thick chilli paste that contains red chilli peppers, sticky rice, fermented soybeans and sweeteners. Heat levels of gochujang can vary and are displayed on the container with a spice indicator. Once gochujang is opened, it must be stored in an airtight container in the refrigerator.

Hoisin sauce is a sweet, thick sauce used in Chinese cuisine, especially BBQ, made from fermented soybeans and Chinese five-spice powder. It can be used for cooking or just as a dipping sauce. Hoisin sauce can be stored in the pantry until opened. Once opened, store in a refrigerator.

Kashmiri chilli powder is made from the Kashmiri chilli that has been dried and ground. Kashmiri chilli has a mild heat with a vibrant red colouring. A good substitute for Kashmiri chilli powder includes paprika or another mild chilli.

Miso is a Japanese paste made from fermented soybeans. Miso comes in several varieties including white (the mildest flavour) and red (allowed to age for longer, making it saltier and with a stronger flavour). Miso can be stored in an airtight container in the refrigerator.

Nori is a dried, edible sheet of seaweed used in Japanese cuisine. It is most commonly used to wrap sushi rolls. Nori can be stored in a cool pantry.

Plantains are related to bananas but are much starchier and can't be eaten raw. Unripe plantains will be green in colour. As they ripen, they turn yellow (medium) and eventually black (fully ripe).

Rice paper is a super-thin wrapper made from rice and used in Vietnamese cuisine. The sheets are dry and need to be rehydrated before use as a wrapper.

Strawberry powder is dehydrated strawberries that have been blended into a powder. You can find this product easily online, or you can use dehydrated strawberries that you grind into a fine powder with a food processor.

Thai basil is a herb with purple stems and green leaves used in Southeast Asian cuisine. It has a liquorice-like and mildly spicy flavour. It is a slightly sturdier herb than Italian basil and is more stable at higher cooking temperatures. Thai basil can be substituted with any type of basil, but it will have a different flavour profile.

Tonkatsu sauce is a thick, sweet sauce used in Japanese cuisine. It can be stored in the pantry. Once opened, it can be stored in the refrigerator in an airtight container for about 2 months.

Umeboshi are pickled plums used in Japanese cuisine. They are extremely sour and salty.

Vanilla pods are commonly used to flavour recipes by slicing them open and scraping the insides. You can substitute 1 tablespoon of vanilla extract or vanilla paste per pod.

Vital wheat gluten is wheat flour that has had most of its starch removed, leaving the wheat proteins behind. The protein content is between 75 and 85 per cent. Adding it to a dough will yield a much more elastic and chewier texture.

Allergy Notes

Just as all Pokémon have their own strengths and weaknesses, people have their own personal tastes and food restrictions. It is important when cooking that you are ready to make adjustments in order to avoid any food allergies. Keep in mind restrictions and accommodations for yourself and any guests you may be feeding. It's always fine to make adjustments to fit the recipes to your own needs.

Adapting to Vegetarian Diets

Most of the recipes in this book are vegetarian or vegan friendly. The remaining two recipes can be adapted to your dietary needs. Swap out proteins with your favourite grilled vegetable or meat substitute. This will affect the cooking times, so plan ahead. Many of the vegetarian dishes can also be adjusted to become vegan by simply using dairy or honey alternatives.

Adapting to Gluten-Free Diets

For most recipes, you can use equal ratios of gluten substitute for flour, but be prepared to modify the quantity just in case the consistency seems off compared to how they are described in the recipes.

Adapting to Lactose-Free Diets

Feel free to replace milk and double cream with your favourite non-dairy milk. There are also plenty of butter alternatives that work well to replace butter in recipes. Replacing butter with oil isn't always the best choice, as it doesn't give the same consistency needed for certain recipes. If you do use oil instead, add it in smaller batches to check the consistency as you go.

Poké Ball

Dusk Ball

Fast Ball

Poké Ball Poke Bowls

Poké Balls are all useful in the right circumstances. A Pokémon Trainer needs to be prepared, so let's prepare our own poke bowls. Try making your Poké Ball shapes with some of your favourite ingredients!

Difficulty: ● ● ○ ○
Prep Time: 45 minutes
Rest Time: 1 hour
Cook Time: 15 minutes
Yield: 6 servings

Equipment: Rice cooker, chopping board, knife, small non-stick pan, bowls

Sushi Rice
4 cups (840 grams) sushi rice
Water
2 tablespoons rice vinegar
1 tablespoon sugar
½ teaspoon rock salt

note: Make sure to follow the ratios of your rice cooker. Measure with the cup it came with and add the amount of water it recommends.

Poké Ball
2 tablespoons soy sauce
2 teaspoons sesame oil
1 teaspoon rice vinegar
1 teaspoon grated fresh ginger
1 spring onion, white and light green parts finely chopped
12 ounces (340 grams) sushi-grade tuna, cubed
¼ to ½ portion of the cooked sushi rice
1 sheet nori

Sushi Rice

1. Put the rice in a bowl, fill it with cold water and rub in a circular motion. The water will become opaque, which means the rice still needs to be cleaned. Strain the water out and repeat until the water is clear.

2. Place the cleaned rice and the amount of water required into a rice cooker and allow the rice to cook.

3. When the rice is done cooking, remove from the rice cooker and place inside a non-metallic bowl.

4. In a small bowl, combine the rice vinegar, sugar and salt. Add the vinegar mixture to the rice while the rice is still hot. Take a spatula and fold in the vinegar mixture. Continue to fold and slice the rice until it has cooled down.

Poké Ball

1. Combine the soy sauce, sesame oil, rice vinegar, ginger and spring onions in an airtight container. Whisk together until well combined. Add the tuna and stir to combine. Seal the container and place in the refrigerator. Let the tuna rest in the refrigerator for 30 minutes and up to 1 hour.

2. To serve, take two bowls and place a serving of sushi rice in each. Top the top half of each with the tuna. Use a piece of nori to create the black line in the centre of the Poké Ball.

Dusk Ball

Dusk Ball

16 ounces (450 grams) seedless watermelon, cubed

3 tablespoons soy sauce

1 lime, zested and juiced

2 teaspoons sesame oil

2 teaspoons rice vinegar

1 teaspoon grated fresh ginger

1 teaspoon sugar

¼ to ½ portion of the cooked sushi rice

½ cup (80 grams) edamame

1 avocado, thinly sliced

1 sheet nori

1. Heat a small non-stick pan over a medium heat. Add the watermelon and cook until it is no longer releasing liquid, about 5 to 8 minutes. Remove from the heat and allow to cool completely.

2. Combine the soy sauce, lime juice and zest, sesame oil, rice vinegar, ginger and sugar in an airtight container. Whisk together until well combined. Add the watermelon and stir to combine. Seal the container and place in the refrigerator. Let the watermelon rest in the refrigerator for at least 1 hour, but overnight is best.

3. To serve, take two bowls and place a serving of sushi rice in each. Cover the top half of each with edamame. Cover the bottom half with sliced avocado. Use a piece of shaped nori to create the black lines of the Dusk Ball. Finally, place a row of watermelon in the centre.

Fast Ball

Fast Ball

2 tablespoons soy sauce

2 teaspoons sesame oil

1 teaspoon rice vinegar

1 teaspoon grated fresh ginger

1 spring onion, white and light green parts finely chopped

12 ounces (340 grams) sushi-grade salmon, cubed

¼ to ½ portion of the cooked sushi rice

1 mango, peeled and thinly sliced

1 sheet nori

1. Combine the soy sauce, sesame oil, rice vinegar, ginger and spring onions in an airtight container. Whisk together until well combined. Add the salmon and stir to combine. Seal the container and place in the refrigerator. Let the salmon rest in the refrigerator for 30 minutes and up to 1 hour.

2. To serve, take two bowls and place a serving of sushi rice in each. Top the top half of each with the salmon. Place slices of mango on the sides to make the Fast Ball. Use a piece of nori to create the black line in the centre.

Kanto Region

Charizard
Pikachu
Gengar
Seaking
Dragonite

Charizard
Spicy Arrabbiata

This spicy arrabbiata is full of flavour and heat. Eat enough of it, and you may be able to blow flames just like Charizard! But breathe fire carefully if you do.

Difficulty: ● ○ ○ ○
Prep Time: 30 minutes
Cook Time: 45 minutes
Yield: 4 servings

Equipment: Large non-stick pan, chopping board, knife, cheese grater

3 tablespoons olive oil
5 garlic cloves, crushed
2 tablespoons tomato paste
1 teaspoon sweet paprika
1 teaspoon dried chilli flakes
4 to 6 Calabrian chilli peppers, chopped
1 large lemon, zested
One 28-ounce (2x 400-gram) can plum tomatoes
2 teaspoons sugar
¼ cup (25 grams) Pecorino Romano, grated, plus more for serving
16 ounces (450 grams) tagliatelle, cooked and 1/2 cup (120 millilitres) cooking water reserved
Rock salt
Ground black pepper
Fresh basil

1. Combine the olive oil, garlic and tomato paste in a large non-stick pan. Heat over a medium heat. Cook for 5 minutes until the garlic just starts to brown. Add the paprika, chilli flakes, Calabrian chilli peppers and lemon zest.

2. Crush the plum tomatoes with your hands and add them to the pan. Add the sugar and Pecorino Romano and mix everything together. Reduce the heat to a medium-low and simmer for 30 minutes.

3. Add the cooked pasta to the sauce and mix together. If too thick, add cooking water to loosen. Season with salt and pepper. Serve with fresh basil and extra Pecorino Romano.

Pikachu
Lemon Tarts

These lemon tarts are the perfect dessert to enjoy with your best friends. You can't exchange electricity with friends like Pikachu can, but you can share these shockingly tart treats.

Difficulty: ● ● ○ ○
Prep Time: 1 hour
Rest Time: 3 hours
Cook Time: 30 minutes
Yield: 12 tarts

Equipment: Food processor, 4-inch (10-centimetre) tart tins, rolling pin, large baking sheet, baking paper, pie weights, medium saucepan, spatula, wire rack

Tart Shells
1½ cups (240 grams) plain flour
½ cup (70 grams) icing sugar
½ teaspoon rock salt
4 ounces (110 grams) unsalted butter, cubed and chilled
2 egg yolks
1/2 lemon, zested
1 teaspoon vanilla extract
1 tablespoon milk

Lemon Curd
6 egg yolks
1¼ cups (250 grams) sugar
1 lemon, zested
²⁄₃ cup (160 millilitres) lemon juice
1 pinch rock salt
6 ounces (165 grams) unsalted butter
2 drops yellow food colouring (optional)

For assembly
Fresh raspberries for decorating
White, black and yellow candy melts for decorating

To make the tart shells

1. Combine the flour, icing sugar and salt in a food processor. Add the cubed butter. Pulse until the mixture resembles breadcrumbs with a few chunks of butter.

2. Add the egg yolks, lemon zest, vanilla extract and milk. Pulse until the dough comes together. Remove the dough from the food processor and lightly knead to bring it all together. Split into two portions. Wrap in cling film and place in the refrigerator for at least 1 hour.

3. Take one of the dough portions and split it into six pieces. Take one of the pieces and roll it out to the size of your tart tin. Carefully lay the dough into the tin and remove any excess. Prick the bottom of the tart with a fork and place on a large baking sheet. Repeat with the remaining dough pieces. Place the baking sheet with the tarts in the freezer for 10 minutes before baking.

note: If you only have a few small tart tins, you can do this and the baking steps in smaller batches. Just make sure to leave any unused dough in the refrigerator until your tins are ready to use again.

4. Preheat the oven to 375°F (190°C). Place a small piece of baking paper on top of each of the crusts. Fill with pie weights (or dry beans) to help keep the crust from rising. Bake for 13 minutes.

5. Take the tarts out and remove the baking paper and weights. Place back in the oven and bake until the crust is golden brown, about 3 to 5 minutes. Allow to cool slightly before removing from the tins and letting cool completely on a wire rack.

continued on the next page

To make the lemon curd

1. In a medium saucepan, whisk the egg yolks, sugar and lemon zest until the sugar dissolves and the mixture is smooth. Add the lemon juice and salt. Place over a low heat and whisk until it becomes thick, about 10 minutes.

   note: To test if the curd is thick enough, dip a spoon in the mixture and run a finger across the back of it. If the trail holds, it is OK! Keep in mind the curd will continue to thicken as it cools.

2. Add the butter and yellow food colouring. Whisk until the butter is completely melted. Allow to cool for 10 minutes.

3. Carefully pour the curd into the cooled tart crust. If there are any major bubbles in the curd, use a cocktail stick to pop them. Place in a deep dish and cover, making sure the curd is not being touched by anything, so it doesn't stick as it cools.

4. Place in the refrigerator for at least 1 hour before serving. The curd can be refrigerated for up to 1 week.

5. Prepare a baking sheet with baking paper. Begin by preparing the eyes. Place white candy melts in a piping bag. Heat in the microwave for 30 seconds to 1 minute, until the candy melt is melted.

6. Cut the end of the piping bag and shape small white rounds for the white part of Pikachu's eye on the prepared baking paper. Make twenty-four of these in total.

7. Place black candy melts in a piping bag. Heat in the microwave for 30 seconds to 1 minute, until the candy melt is melted.

8. Cut the end of the piping bag and carefully spread the black over the already set white pieces to finish Pikachu's eyes. Repeat until you have twenty-four eyes in total.

9. For the ears, form the top black portion of the ears on the baking paper. Repeat this until you have twenty-four of these shapes. Place yellow candy melts in a piping bag. Heat in the microwave for 30 seconds to 1 minute, until the candy melt is melted.

10. Cut the end of the piping bag and shape the yellow part of Pikachu's ears on the prepared black tips. Repeat until you have twenty-four ear pieces.

11. Use the remaining melted black chocolate to shape Pikachu's mouth and nose. When placing these prepared candy melts on the tarts make sure to have the smooth bottom side face up.

To assemble Pikachu's face:

Create the eyes, mouth, nose and ears with melted candy melts that have cooled and set. Place two raspberries for Pikachu's red cheeks.

Gengar
Yoghurt Bowl

This yoghurt bowl has a deep purple colour like Gengar and is full of delicious nuts and fruit. You may feel chilly when working with the frozen fruit, but it's probably not a Gengar lurking in the shadows watching you cook.

Difficulty: ● ● ○ ○
Prep Time: 30 minutes
Rest Time: 45 minutes
Cook Time: 30 minutes
Yield: 1 to 2 bowls

Equipment: Large bowl, spatula, small saucepan, medium baking sheet, baking paper, blender

Granola

3 cups (360 grams) old-fashioned rolled oats
½ cup (55 grams) walnuts, chopped
½ cup (55 grams) pecans, chopped
4 ounces (110 grams) unsalted butter
⅓ cup (110 grams) honey
3 tablespoons brown sugar
½ teaspoon ground cardamom
½ teaspoon rock salt
1 vanilla pod, seeds scraped and pod discarded
½ cup (70 grams) dried cherries
¼ cup (40 grams) dried blueberries

Berry Yoghurt Mixture

1 cup (240 grams) plain yoghurt
¾ cup (140 grams) frozen blueberries
½ cup (90 grams) frozen blackberries
1 banana

For assembly, per bowl

½ cup (75 grams) granola
Berry yoghurt for serving
Shredded coconut flakes for garnishing
Fresh strawberries for garnishing

To make the granola:

1. Preheat the oven to 350°F (175°C). Prepare a medium baking sheet with baking paper. Combine the rolled oats, walnuts and pecans in a large bowl. Set aside.

2. Combine the butter, honey, brown sugar, ground cardamom, salt and vanilla pod seeds in a small saucepan. Place over a medium heat and mix until the butter has melted and the sugar has dissolved. Carefully pour this into the large bowl with the oat mixture. Mix until well combined.

3. Transfer to the baking sheet and spread into a thin layer. Place in the oven and bake for 10 minutes. Stir and bake for another 10 minutes, or until golden brown. Remove from the oven and let cool for 45 minutes. Once cooled, transfer to an airtight container. Mix in the dried cherries and blueberries. This can be stored at room temperature in an airtight container for 10 days. This makes enough granola for about ten portions.

To make the berry yoghurt mixture:

Place the yoghurt, frozen blueberries, frozen blackberries and banana in a blender. Blend until smooth.

For assembly:

Place the granola at the bottom of a bowl. Add the berry yoghurt. Top with coconut flakes, strawberries and additional granola to your liking.

Seaking
Dragon Fruit Agua Fresca

Agua fresca is a delicious, refreshing drink that works all year round. But the perfect time to enjoy this drink is during autumn. Add the ice cubes and watch the drink turn a pretty shade of red.

Difficulty: ●○○○
Prep Time: 10 minutes
Rest Time: 8 hours
Yield: 4 to 6 servings

Equipment: Blender, large jug, ice cube tray

Citrus Ice Cubes
2 grapefruits, juiced
1 blood orange, juiced
2 limes, juiced
½ cup (120 millilitres) water
2 tablespoons grenadine

Dragon Fruit Agua Fresca
3 dragon fruits (white flesh)
3 cups (710 millilitres) coconut water
¼ cup (50 grams) sugar
3 limes, juiced

To make the citrus ice cubes:
Combine all of the ingredients in a large cup. Transfer to an ice cube tray. Place in the freezer for at least 8 hours before serving.

note: These ice cubes will be slightly softer than normal ice cubes.

To make the dragon fruit agua fresca:
1. Remove the skin of the dragon fruit. Cut up the interior and transfer to a blender. Add the coconut water, sugar and lime juice. Blend until smooth. Transfer to a large jug.

2. Taste and add additional lime juice if needed. Store in the refrigerator for 30 minutes to chill. The agua fresca can be stored for up to 3 days in the refrigerator.

3. To serve, add 3 citrus ice cubes to a large glass. Shake the agua fresca if it has separated and pour into the prepared glass.

Dragonite
Butternut Squash Gnocchi

Kind-hearted Dragonite simply must help people in need. After a bite of this gnocchi, you'll find yourself equally determined to help yourself to another serving of this delectable dish.

Difficulty: ● ● ○ ○
Prep Time: 30 minutes
Cook Time: 2 hours
Yield: 4 servings

Equipment: Chopping board, knife, large baking sheet, blender, large saucepan, large non-stick pan

½ butternut squash, halved and seeded
1 tablespoon olive oil, plus more for greasing
Rock salt
1 onion, chopped
4 garlic cloves, chopped
1 tablespoon shiro miso
½ teaspoon dried sage
1 ½ cups (360 millilitres) coconut milk
17 ounces (480 grams) pre-made gnocchi
2 ounces (55 grams) unsalted butter
10 fresh sage leaves, roughly chopped

1. Preheat the oven to 375°F (190°C). Place the butternut squash (open side up) on a large baking sheet. Rub with olive oil and generously season with salt. Place in the oven and bake for 1 to 1½ hours, until the butternut squash is tender. Remove from the oven and allow to cool. Once cooled, carefully peel away the skin and place the flesh in a blender.

2. Place a large non-stick pan over a medium-high heat. Add the olive oil and allow to heat up. Add the onion and cook until softened, about 5 minutes. Add the garlic and cook until softened, about 2 minutes. Remove from the heat and transfer to the blender.

3. Add the shiro miso, dried sage and coconut milk to the blender. Blend until smooth. Set aside until the gnocchi is prepared.

note: The sauce should be relatively thick but not so thick that the blender can't blend all the ingredients together. If the mixture is too thick, add additional coconut milk.

4. Heat a large saucepan with water and salt over a high heat. Bring to the boil and cook the gnocchi to the package's instructions. Reserve 2 cups (480 millilitres) of the water and drain the gnocchi.

5. Heat a large non-stick pan over a medium-high heat. Add half the butter and allow to melt. Add the gnocchi and pan fry until they are golden brown, about 2 minutes per side. Transfer to four serving plates.

6. Add the remaining butter to the pan and let it melt. Add the fresh sage until it turns slightly brown, about 2 minutes. Transfer to another plate.

7. Add the blended butternut squash and cook until heated through. If the sauce becomes too thick, add a bit of the reserved water and mix in well. Top each of the plates of gnocchi with sauce and sprinkle with the sage.

Johto Region

Furret
Ampharos
Shuckle
Umbreon
Swinub
Miltank

Furret
Fluffy Pancakes

Furret is fluffy and able to squeeze into narrow spaces when it needs to get away. These pancakes are also fluffy and have the same rings as Furret's tail. If you eat too many, you won't be feeling as nimble as Furret.

Difficulty: ● ● ○ ○
Prep Time: 30 minutes
Rest Time: 20 minutes
Cook Time: 10 minutes per batch
Yield: 4 to 6 servings

Equipment: Medium bowl, large bowl, whisk, medium non-stick pan

Vanilla Cardamom Pancakes

1 cup (160 grams) plain flour
½ teaspoon ground cardamom
¼ teaspoon ground cinnamon
2 tablespoons sugar
½ vanilla pod, seeds scraped and pod discarded
1 teaspoon baking powder
½ teaspoon bicarbonate of soda
1 pinch rock salt
1 egg, separated
¾ cup (180 millilitres) buttermilk
1 ounce (30 grams) unsalted butter, melted and cooled
1 teaspoon vanilla extract
Non-stick cooking spray for greasing

Chocolate Pancakes

1 cup (160 grams) plain flour
1 tablespoon cocoa powder
2 tablespoons sugar
1 teaspoon baking powder
½ teaspoon bicarbonate of soda
1 pinch rock salt
1 egg, separated
¾ cup (180 millilitres) buttermilk
1 ounce (30 grams) unsalted butter, melted and cooled
½ teaspoon vanilla extract
Non-stick cooking spray for greasing
Black candy melts for decorating (optional)

Vanilla Cardamom Pancakes

1. Combine the flour, cardamom, cinnamon, sugar, vanilla pod seeds, baking powder, bicarbonate of soda and salt in a medium bowl. Place the egg white in a large bowl. Whisk until the egg white becomes frothy.

2. Add the egg yolk, buttermilk, melted butter and vanilla extract to the egg white. Add the dry ingredients and fold in until the mixture just comes together. Set aside and let rest for 20 minutes at room temperature.

3. Heat a medium non-stick pan over a medium heat and spray with non-stick cooking spray. Take a cup of the batter and pour it into the pan. Allow the pancake to cook. The pancake is ready to flip once you begin to see small bubbles at the top, about 3 to 5 minutes. Flip the pancake and allow it to cook until the other side is golden brown, about another 2 minutes. Repeat with the remaining batter.

Chocolate Pancakes

1. Combine the flour, cocoa powder, sugar, baking powder, bicarbonate of soda and salt in a medium bowl. Place the egg white in a large bowl. Whisk until the egg white becomes frothy.

2. Add the egg yolk, buttermilk, melted butter and vanilla extract to the egg white. Add the dry ingredients and fold in until the mixture just comes together. Set aside and let rest for 20 minutes at room temperature.

3. Heat a medium non-stick pan over a medium heat and spray with non-stick cooking spray. Take a cup of the batter and pour it into the pan. Allow the pancake to cook. The pancake is ready to flip once you begin to see small bubbles at the top, about 3 to 5 minutes. Flip the pancake and allow it to cook until the other side is golden brown, about another 2 minutes. Repeat with the remaining batter.

4. To serve, alternate the pancakes on a plate to match Furret's fur pattern. Make little eyes, cheek markings and a mouth with candy melts. Place on the top pancake and enjoy.

note: Feel free to add whipped cream or syrup for dipping!

Ampharos
Lemonade

The light from Ampharos's tail is so bright that it can be seen from space! This lemonade isn't quite so bright, but it makes for a perfect thirst quencher.

Difficulty: ● ○ ○ ○
Prep Time: 15 minutes
Rest Time: 8 hours
Cook Time: 10 minutes
Yield: 4 servings

Equipment: Small saucepan, large jug, ice cube tray

Lemon Ice Cubes
3 lemons, juiced
2 lemons, zested

Simple Syrup
½ cup (120 millilitres) water
½ cup (100 grams) sugar
2 lemons, zested

Lemonade
¾ cup (180 millilitres) lemon juice (about 3 to 5 lemons)
2 to 3 cups (480 to 720 millilitres) water

To make the lemon ice cubes:
Combine all of the ingredients in a large cup. Transfer to an ice cube tray. Place in the freezer for at least 8 hours before serving.

note: These ice cubes will be slightly softer than normal ice cubes.

To make the simple syrup:
Combine the water and sugar in a small saucepan and place over a medium-high heat. Whisk until the sugar has dissolved and bring to a boil. Reduce the heat and add the lemon zest. Simmer for 5 minutes. Remove the syrup from the heat and let cool to room temperature.

To make the lemonade:
In a large jug, combine the simple syrup, lemon juice and water. Mix together. Store in the refrigerator for at least 3 hours before serving. The lemonade can be stored in the refrigerator for up to 7 days.

Shuckle
Berry Juice

Shuckle likes to store berries in its shell where they eventually ferment into a delicious juice. Instead of waiting for a Shuckle, we can get our own berries and make juice just as delicious for ourselves.

Difficulty: ● ○ ○ ○
Prep Time: 10 minutes
Yield: 2 servings

Equipment: Blender

1 banana
10 frozen strawberries
30 frozen raspberries
5 frozen blueberries
1 cup (245 grams) frozen vanilla yoghurt
¼ to ½ cup (59 to 118 millilitres) pomegranate juice

Place the banana and frozen berries in the blender. Blend until smooth. Add the frozen vanilla yoghurt and a ¼ cup of pomegranate juice and blend. If too thick, add more pomegranate juice.

Umbreon
Dark Chocolate Bagels

When Umbreon gets angry, it can secrete poison to ward off others. Although this bagel is perfectly fine to eat, it also has a strong bite that goes great with some yellow sweetened cream cheese.

Difficulty: ● ● ● ○
Prep Time: 1 hour
Rest Time: 12 hours
Cook Time: 25 minutes
Yield: 6 bagels

Equipment: Small bowl, large bowl, large baking sheet, baking paper, large saucepan

Sweetened Cream Cheese

8 ounces (225 grams) cream cheese, room temperature
4 drops yellow food colouring (optional)
½ vanilla pod, seeds scraped and pod discarded
¼ cup (50 grams) sugar

Bagels

1 cup (240 millilitres) water, heated between 105° and 110°F (40° and 45°C)
1 tablespoon honey
2 ounces (55 grams) dark chocolate, melted
3 drops black food colouring (optional)
2¾ cups (385 grams) bread flour
1 tablespoon dark cocoa powder
1 tablespoon vital wheat gluten
2 teaspoons active dry yeast
2 teaspoons rock salt

Water Bath

8 cups (920 millilitres) water
3 tablespoons honey

Egg Wash

1 egg
1 tablespoon (15 millilitres) water

Sweetened Cream Cheese

Combine all the ingredients together until smooth. Cream cheese can be stored in an airtight container in the refrigerator for up to 2 weeks.

Bagels

1. Combine the water, honey, dark chocolate and black food colouring in a small bowl. Whisk until the honey is dissolved.

2. Combine the bread flour, dark cocoa powder, vital wheat gluten, yeast and salt in a large bowl. Add the water mixture to the dry ingredients and mix until it just comes together. Once combined, let sit for 5 minutes.

3. Transfer to a worktop and knead for about 10 minutes. If the dough is still sticky, add additional flour. The end result will be a very firm dough. Place in an oiled bowl and cover. Let rest in the refrigerator overnight, at least 12 hours.

4. Remove the dough from the refrigerator and split into six equal portions and form into balls. Cover with a kitchen towel and let rest for 20 minutes. Prepare a large baking sheet with baking paper.

5. Take one of the dough balls and roll out flat until it is about 1 inch (2.5 centimetres) thick. Take one end and tightly roll the dough into a log.

6. Using your hands, roll the log until it is about 9 inches (23 centimetres) long. The ends should be slightly thinner than the centre of the log.

7. Take the log and loop it around your hand. The ends should overlap with one another, about 2 to 3 inches (5 to 7 centimetres). Pinch it together. With your hand in the centre of the bagel, carefully roll the two ends together on the counter until they just come together.

8. Transfer to the baking sheet and repeat with the remaining dough portions. Cover and let rest for another 30 minutes. Preheat the oven to 425°F (220°C).

To make the water bath

Combine the water and honey in a large saucepan. Bring to the boil. Place the bagels, but do not overcrowd, in the boiling water for 30 seconds per side and then place back on the baking sheet.

To make the egg wash

Whisk together the egg and water. Brush each bagel with the egg wash. Bake for 18 to 20 minutes, turning halfway through. Serve with the sweetened cream cheese.

Swinub
Truffles

Swinub may not look fast, but they'll go dashing off at the first scent of something enticing. If you make these decadent truffles, be sure to hide them, or you may have a sudden swarm of Swinub on your hands!

Difficulty: ● ● ○ ○
Prep Time: 30 minutes
Rest Time: 4 hours
Cook Time: 5 minutes
Yield: 24 to 30 truffles

Equipment: Chopping board, knife, medium bowl, medium saucepan, spatula, medium baking sheet, baking paper, small bowl

14 ounces (395 grams) dark chocolate, chopped
1 ounce (30 grams) unsalted butter, room temperature
½ cup (120 millilitres) double cream
½ cup (155 grams) chocolate hazelnut spread
2 tablespoons honey
1 pinch rock salt
3 tablespoons cocoa powder

1. Place 12 ounces (340 grams) of the chopped chocolate in a medium bowl. Place the butter and double cream in a medium saucepan and heat over a low heat. Once the butter has melted and the cream is heated to just before a boil, pour over the chopped chocolate. Whisk together until smooth. If the chocolate does not completely melt, place in the microwave for 10 seconds at a time.

2. Mix in the chocolate hazelnut spread, honey and salt. Allow to cool completely before placing in the refrigerator for 3 hours to solidify.

3. Prepare a medium baking sheet with baking paper. Place the cocoa powder in a small bowl. Scoop out 1 tablespoon of the set chocolate. Roll between your hands to form a ball. Place in the bowl with the cocoa powder and toss to coat. Transfer to the baking sheet. Repeat with the remaining chocolate.

note: If the chocolate becomes too warm to handle, place it back in the refrigerator for a couple of minutes to cool.

4. Place the remaining 2 ounces (55 grams) of dark chocolate in a piping bag. Place in a microwave and heat until melted. Cut a small hole at the bottom and create the strips to match Swinub's fur pattern. Take your time with this because the chocolate might slip and slide off as you are placing it. Use a cocktail stick to help place the chocolate back on the truffle.

5. Once the truffles are decorated, place the baking sheet in the refrigerator for 1 hour. Transfer the truffles to an airtight container and store in the refrigerator for up to 2 weeks.

Miltank
Milk Bread

Miltank's highly nutritious milk changes flavours with the season. Let's take some milk and make a fluffy milk bread with different flavours to match!

Difficulty: ● ● ○ ○
Prep Time: 30 minutes
Rest Time: 2 hours
Cook Time: 40 minutes
Yield: 2 loaves

Equipment: Small saucepan, stand mixer with dough hook attachment, 2 large bowls, small bowl, 2 loaf tins, tin foil

Egg wash
1 egg
2 tablespoons milk

Vanilla Dough
Tangzhong
2 tablespoons bread flour
$^1/_3$ cup (80 millilitres) milk

Dough
1 tablespoon active dry yeast
¾ cup (177 millilitres) warm milk
3 cups (420 grams) bread flour
1 teaspoon rock salt
½ vanilla pod, seeds scraped and pod discarded
$^1/_3$ cup (65 grams) sugar
1 teaspoon vanilla extract
1 egg, room temperature
5 tablespoons unsalted butter, softened

Strawberry Dough
Tangzhong
2 tablespoons bread flour
$^1/_3$ cup (80 millilitres) milk

Dough
1 tablespoon active dry yeast
¼ cup (40 grams) strawberry powder
2 drops pink food colouring (optional)
¾ cup (180 millilitres) warm milk
3 cups (430 grams) bread flour
1 teaspoon rock salt
$^1/_3$ cup (65 grams) sugar
1 egg, room temperature
5 tablespoons unsalted butter, softened

Vanilla Dough
To make the tangzhong:
Place the bread flour and milk in a small saucepan over a medium-high heat. Whisk until it comes together, about 1 minute. Set aside and allow to cool.

To make the dough:
1. Combine the yeast and milk and let it rest for 5 minutes, allowing the yeast to become active.

2. Combine the bread flour, salt, vanilla pod seeds and sugar in the bowl of a stand mixer. Add the tangzhong, yeast mixture, vanilla extract and egg to the bowl and mix until it just comes together.

3. While the dough begins to knead, add 1 tablespoon of butter at a time. Knead the dough for 5 minutes. If the dough is too sticky, add 1 tablespoon of flour at a time. If it is too dry, add 1 tablespoon of milk at a time.

4. Transfer to an oiled bowl, cover and let rest for 1 hour, or until it has doubled in size.

Strawberry Dough
To make the tangzhong:
Place the bread flour and milk in a small saucepan over a medium-high heat. Whisk until it comes together, about 1 minute. Set aside and allow to cool.

To make the dough:
1. Combine the yeast, strawberry powder, pink food colouring and milk and let rest for 5 minutes, allowing the yeast to become active.

2. Combine the bread flour, salt and sugar in the bowl of a stand mixer. Add the tangzhong, yeast mixture and egg to the bowl and mix until it just comes together.

3. While the dough begins to knead, add the butter 1 tablespoon at a time. Knead the dough for 5 minutes. If the dough is too sticky, add 1 tablespoon of flour at a time. If it is too dry, add 1 tablespoon of milk at a time.

4. Transfer to an oiled bowl, cover and let rest for 1 hour, or until it has doubled in size.

continued on the next page

For assembly and baking:

1. Once both doughs have doubled in size, punch down and knead. Split each dough into three equal portions. You will have three vanilla dough balls and three strawberry dough balls. Grease two loaf tins.

2. For the first loaf, take one of the strawberry portions and roll the dough out into a long rectangle. Make sure the width of the rolled-out portion is not wider than the baking tin you are using. Carefully roll up the dough. Place in one of the prepared baking pans. Take a vanilla portion and repeat the process. Place the vanilla portion next to the strawberry. Take another strawberry portion, repeat the process and place next to the vanilla portion.

3. Repeat step 2 for the second loaf.

> **note:** The first loaf will be two parts strawberry and one part vanilla, while the second loaf will be two parts vanilla and one part strawberry. I like to alternate the two flavours to make a colourful loaf.

4. Cover and allow to rise again for 45 minutes, or until it doubles in size. Preheat the oven to 350°F (175°C).

5. In a small bowl, combine the egg and milk for the egg wash. Brush the top of the loaves with the egg wash. Place in the oven and bake for 15 minutes. Lightly cover each of the loaves with tin foil to avoid browning too much. Cook for another 15 to 25 minutes, until cooked through.

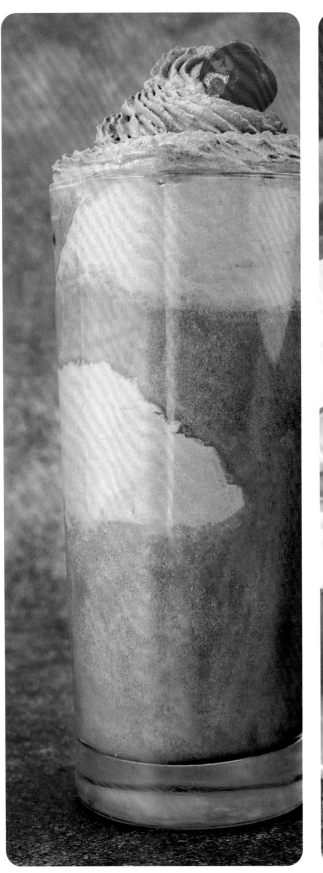

Hoenn Region

Marshtomp
Umeboshi Onigiri

Marshtomp loves playing in the mud on beaches during low tide. Try to mould these onigiri after Marshtomp, capturing the joy it has for getting muddy and sliding around!

Difficulty: ● ● ● ○
Prep Time: 40 minutes
Cook Time: 45 minutes
Yield: 10 onigiri

Equipment: Rice cooker, sieve (optional), medium non-metallic bowl, small bowl, spatula

Blue Sushi Rice
2 cups (420 grams) sushi rice
12 butterfly pea flowers (or blue food colouring)
Water (follow your rice cooker's directions)
2 tablespoons rice vinegar
1 tablespoon sugar
½ teaspoon rock salt

For Assembly
10 orange umeboshi, halved
1 small carrot, peeled
Black sesame seeds for decorating
Pickled ginger for decorating
Nori sheets for decorating

To make the blue sushi rice:

1. Place the rice in a bowl and cover with cold water. With your hands, rub the rice in a circular motion. The water will become opaque. Strain the water and repeat until the water is clear.

> **note:** You can use a sieve to help you with the draining process to avoid losing any rice grains. One option is to put the rice in the sieve and place it in the bowl. Fill with water, rub, remove the sieve from the bowl, pour out the water and repeat.

2. Place the cleaned rice, butterfly pea flowers and amount of water required into a rice cooker and allow the rice to cook. When the rice is done, remove from the rice cooker and place inside a medium non-metallic bowl. Remove the butterfly pea flowers.

3. Combine the rice vinegar, sugar and salt in a small bowl. Add the vinegar mixture to the rice while the rice is still hot. Take a spatula and fold in the rice vinegar. Continue to fold and slice the rice until it has cooled down.

> **note:** You can also add a drop or two of light blue food colouring to the vinegar mixture in order to make the colour pop more. It's a good idea to wait until the rice is done cooking to make that decision.

To assemble the onigiri:

1. Have a small bowl of water to keep your hands moist during the process. Wet your hands and then take a handful of the rice mixture and begin forming large oval shapes. Use a moderate amount of pressure to make sure they are formed correctly.

2. Take two umeboshi halves and place them on the sides for Marshtomp's cheeks. Place one small, julienned carrot slice in the centre of each umeboshi and pierce through to the rice.

3. To shape the eyes, take two small carrot slices and shape into an oval matching Marshtomp's eye shape. Carefully take a black sesame seed and wet it. Place in the centre of the carrot.

4. Take a piece of pickled ginger to shape the mouth. Take a second piece and cut it to make the tongue. Finally, top with a piece of nori to match the top fin.

Breloom
Spring Rolls

If you want to put a spring to your step just like Breloom, why not enjoy some spring rolls? They are light and flavourful, and will keep you feeling refreshed and ready for whatever activities you have planned.

Difficulty: ● ● ● ○
Prep Time: 1 hour
Cook Time: 30 minutes
Yield: 14 spring rolls

Equipment: Chopping board, knife, large bowl, large non-stick pan, deep dish

Spring Rolls
16 ounces (450 grams) firm tofu
Salt
Pepper
¼ cup (35 grams) cornflour
1 teaspoon rapeseed oil
Lukewarm water
14 round rice paper sheets
1 head lettuce
8 ounces (225 grams) rice vermicelli, cooked and cooled
1 cucumber, peeled and cut into long, thin slices
2 carrots, peeled and julienned
1 red bell pepper, thinly sliced
10 radishes, thinly sliced
$\frac{1}{3}$ cup (50 grams) fresh coriander
$\frac{1}{3}$ cup (45 grams) fresh mint
3 ounces (85 grams) fresh Thai basil

Peanut Sauce
¼ cup (90 grams) smooth peanut butter
3 garlic cloves, crushed
1 tablespoon rice vinegar
1 tablespoon soy sauce
3 tablespoons coconut milk
1 lime, juiced
1 tablespoon maple syrup
1 teaspoon sesame oil

To make the spring rolls:

1. Place the tofu between two plates and top with a heavy object. Allow to rest for 5 minutes to remove excess liquid. Cut the tofu into fourteen rectangle pieces. Season with salt and pepper. Toss in the cornflour, covering all sides, and set aside.

2. Heat a large non-stick pan with rapeseed oil over a medium-high heat. Add the tofu and cook until all sides have slightly browned, about 3 minutes per side. Transfer to a plate.

3. Fill a deep dish, large enough to fit a piece of rice paper, with lukewarm water. Soak a rice paper sheet in the dish until it softens slightly. Place on the chopping board.

4. Place a piece of lettuce in the lower half of the rice paper sheet.

5. Add a portion of vermicelli, one piece of tofu, two to three slices of cucumber, a small portion of carrots, one to two slices of red bell pepper, several pieces of radish and the herbs on top of the lettuce.

6. Grab the lower edge of the rice paper and start rolling the lettuce portion. When you just begin to cover all the fillings, about halfway up, tuck the sides inward. Continuing rolling until sealed.

note: The rice paper will get softer and softer as it sits out. Do these one at a time to make sure the rice paper isn't too difficult to wrap up.

To make the peanut sauce:

Combine all the ingredients in a bowl. Serve immediately or store in the refrigerator until you are ready to serve.

Swalot
Ube Flan

Though it may be tempting to imitate Swalot's eating habits and swallow this entire ube flan in one gulp, habits like that are only good for Swalot. You'll enjoy this treat if you take your time and savour every bite.

Difficulty: ● ● ○ ○
Prep Time: 30 minutes
Rest Time: 4 hours
Cook Time: 1 hour
Yield: 6 servings

Equipment: Medium saucepan, 6 3½-inch (9-centimetre) ramekins, large deep baking dish, medium bowl, large bowl, baking paper, large baking sheet

Chocolate Biscuit

1½ cups (240 grams) plain flour
1 tablespoon dark cocoa powder
½ teaspoon rock salt
4 ounces (110 grams) unsalted butter, room temperature
½ cup (100 grams) sugar
1 egg
2 teaspoons vanilla extract

Flan

⅔ cup (140 grams) sugar
¼ cup (60 millilitres) water
1 teaspoon rock salt
3 eggs
2 egg yolks
14 ounces (400 grams) sweetened condensed milk
12 ounces (340 grams) evaporated milk
2 teaspoons ube extract
1 tablespoon vanilla extract

To make the chocolate biscuit:

1. Combine the plain flour, dark cocoa powder and salt in a medium bowl. Cream the butter in a large bowl. Add the sugar and mix until combined and slightly fluffy. Add the egg and vanilla extract. Finally, add the flour mixture and whisk together until it is just combined.

2. Place the dough on a sheet of baking paper. Lightly flour the portion and then cover with another sheet of baking paper. Roll the dough out to ¼ to ½ inch (6 to 13 millimetres) thickness. Cover and place in the refrigerator and let rest for at least 1 hour.

3. Preheat the oven to 350°F (175°C). After the dough has rested, take it out and place it on a floured surface. Carefully cut out the biscuit with a biscuit cutter. Place the cut-out biscuit on a large baking sheet covered in baking paper. Reshape the remaining dough and roll it out once again. Cut out more biscuits. Repeat this until you have used up all the dough. Bake for 8 to 10 minutes, or until the centre is set and firm.

note: This will make many more biscuits than you would need to set up the ube flan.

To make the flan:

1. Preheat the oven to 350°F (175°C). Combine the sugar and water in a medium saucepan over a medium-low heat. Allow to simmer for 15 minutes, until it turns golden. Immediately add the salt and stir in. Pour the caramel from the saucepan into six 3½-inch (9-centimetre) ramekins. Rotate the ramekins around to spread it evenly on the bottom.

2. Combine the whole eggs, egg yolks, sweetened condensed milk, evaporated milk, ube extract and vanilla extract in a medium bowl until smooth. Pour the mixture into the ramekins.

3. Place the ramekins inside a large deep baking dish. Fill the baking dish around the ramekins with water about halfway up the ramekins. Place in the oven and bake for 40 to 50 minutes, or until the internal temperature reaches 175°F (80°C).

4. Remove the ramekins from the baking dish and allow them to cool. Once they are completely cooled, place in a refrigerator for at least 3 hours before serving. To remove them from the ramekins, run a knife along the side, place a plate upside down over the ramekin and flip upright. Serve with the chocolate biscuits.

Spinda
Raspberry Marble Cake

Every Spinda's spot pattern is different. These marble cakes are made with beautiful swirls, so try to make a unique swirl pattern with each!

Difficulty: ● ● ○ ○
Prep Time: 45 minutes
Cook Time: 20 to 25 minutes
Yield: 8 mini cakes

Equipment: Blender, sieve, stand mixer with paddle, medium bowl, 8-hole mini loaf tin, wire rack

4 ounces (110 grams) fresh raspberries
2 drops red food colouring
1 drop orange food colouring
2 cups (320 grams) plain flour
2 teaspoons baking powder
1 teaspoon rock salt
5 ounces (140 grams) unsalted butter, room temperature
1 cup (200 grams) sugar
4 egg whites, room temperature
1 teaspoon vanilla extract
⅔ cup (160 millilitres) buttermilk, room temperature

1. Preheat the oven to 350°F (175°C). Place the raspberries in a blender and purée. Pour the puréed raspberries through a sieve to remove the seeds. Mix in the food colouring and set aside.

2. Combine the plain flour, baking powder and salt in a medium bowl. Set aside. Place the butter in the bowl of a stand mixer and cream until fluffy. Add the sugar and mix until smooth. Add the egg whites and vanilla extract. Mix until combined.

3. Add half of the dry ingredients into the stand mixer and mix. Add the buttermilk and mix until smooth. Add the remaining dry ingredients and mix until just combined.

4. Pour half of the mixture into another bowl. To that bowl, add the puréed raspberries and mix until the colour of the batter is uniform.

5. Prepare the 8-hole mini loaf tin by spraying with non-stick oil. Spoon in each of the batters, alternating to create unique patterns.

note: Make sure you can see some of the vanilla and raspberry batter at the top. Have fun with this and make your own combinations.

6. Place in the oven and bake for 18 to 25 minutes, or until a skewer test comes out clean. Allow to rest for 5 minutes and then remove from the pan onto a wire rack.

Flygon
Avocado Toast

Spotting a Flygon is a rare occurrence. It would rather hide in the heart of a sandstorm than fly around in public. Try to remember what Flygon looks like by making your own on a piece of delicious avocado toast.

Difficulty: ● ○ ○ ○
Prep Time: 30 minutes
Yield: 4 servings

Equipment: Medium bowl, chopping board, knife

4 ounces (110 grams) cream cheese, room temperature

2 tablespoons soured cream

½ tablespoon lemon juice

1/2 lemon, zested

¼ teaspoon rock salt

¼ teaspoon black pepper

1 teaspoon fresh dill leaves

4 slices thick white bread

2 avocados, sliced

1 tomato, sliced

3 spring onions, dark green part only

Pomegranate seeds for garnishing

1. Whisk together the cream cheese and soured cream in a medium bowl. Add the lemon juice, lemon zest, salt, black pepper and dill leaves. Mix until just combined. Place in an airtight container. The cream cheese mixture can be stored in the refrigerator for up to 1 week.

2. Toast the white bread to your liking. Place each of the pieces of toast on a plate and cover with the cream cheese mixture. Top with the avocado, tomato, spring onions and pomegranate seeds.

note: You can use all of these elements to shape the toppings to look just like Flygon.

Relicanth
Chocolate Malt

This chocolate malt has an intense, deep flavour, inspired by Relicanth's natural deep-sea habitat. It's dark and murky but oh so delicious. Don't forget the cherry to match Relicanth's marking!

Difficulty: ● ○ ○ ○
Prep Time: 30 minutes
Yield: 2 malts

Equipment: Stand mixer with whisk attachment, blender

Chocolate Whipped Cream

½ cup (120 millilitres) double cream

2 tablespoons cocoa powder

1 tablespoon icing sugar

Dark Chocolate Malt Layer

1 tablespoon dark cocoa powder

3 tablespoons malted milk powder

¼ cup (60 millilitres) whole milk

11 ounces (310 grams) chocolate ice cream

2 maraschino cherries

To make the chocolate whipped cream:

Place all the ingredients in the bowl of a stand mixer. Mix on a medium-high speed until the whipped cream forms stiff peaks, about 3 to 5 minutes. Transfer to a piping bag and store in the refrigerator until needed.

To make the dark chocolate malt layer:

1. In a blender, add the dark cocoa powder, malted milk powder and milk. Blend until combined. Add the ice cream and blend until smooth. If the mixture is too thick, add a small amount of milk.

2. Pour about halfway up in two large glasses. Take the prepared whipped cream and add a layer of it on top. Add the remaining chocolate malt. Top each with additional whipped cream and a maraschino cherry.

Sinnoh Region

Combee
Drifloon
Munchlax
Abomasnow
Weavile
Froslass

Combee
Honey Biscuits

Combee are a trio, working together all day to gather nectar. When you ice these biscuits, you can make all sorts of Combee faces and combine them for silly groupings.

Difficulty: ● ● ○ ○
Prep Time: 30 minutes
Rest Time: 1 hour
Cook Time: 15 minutes
Yield: 24 biscuits

Equipment: Medium bowl, large bowl, 2 large baking sheets, baking paper, hexagon biscuit cutter

3½ cups (560 grams) plain flour
1 teaspoon ground ginger
1 teaspoon rock salt
8 ounces (225 grams) unsalted butter, room temperature
½ cup (110 grams) sugar
½ cup (165 grams) honey
2 eggs
1 teaspoon vanilla extract
Black candy melts for decorating

1. Combine the flour, ginger and salt in a medium bowl. Cream the butter in a large bowl. Add the sugar and honey. Mix until combined and slightly fluffy. Add the eggs and vanilla extract. Finally, add the flour mixture and whisk together until it is just combined. Split the dough in half.

2. Take one of the halves and transfer onto a sheet of baking paper. Lightly flour the portion and then cover with another sheet of baking paper. Roll the dough out to ¼ to ½ inch (6 to 13 millimetres) thickness. Cover and place in the refrigerator to rest for at least 1 hour. Repeat this step with the other half of the dough.

3. Preheat the oven to 350°F (175°C). After the dough has rested, take one of the halves out and place it on a very floured surface. Carefully use a biscuit cutter to cut out a biscuit. Place the biscuit on a large baking sheet covered with baking paper. Reshape the remaining dough and roll it out once again. Cut out more biscuits. Repeat until you have used up all the of dough. Bake for 12 to 15 minutes, or until golden brown.

4. Allow the biscuits to completely cool before icing them. Use black candy melts to add Combee faces.

Drifloon
Blackberry Marshmallows

These marshmallows are so fluffy and violet, you'd think they would float away just like Drifloon. You could even cut them out in fun Drifloon shapes if you'd like.

Difficulty: ● ● ○ ○
Prep Time: 30 minutes
Rest Time: 24 hours
Cook Time: 15 minutes
Yield: 24 large marshmallows

Equipment: Food processor, sieve, medium saucepan, sugar thermometer, stand mixer with whisk attachment, medium roasting tin

8 ounces (225 grams) fresh blackberries
Cold water
2 tablespoons unflavoured gelatin
3 drops purple food colouring (optional)
1¾ cups (375 grams) sugar
½ cup (165 grams) golden syrup
½ teaspoon rock salt
1 teaspoon vanilla extract
Non-stick cooking spray for greasing
Icing sugar for dusting
Yellow candy melts for decorating
Whipped cream for decorating

1. Place the blackberries in a food processor and blend until smooth. Transfer to a measuring cup by passing the liquid through a sieve to remove any seeds. Add cold water to the measuring cup to have the liquid equal 1 cup (240 millilitres) in total.

2. Pour half of the blackberry mixture into a stand mixer. Add the gelatin and purple food colouring. Whisk everything together and set aside.

3. Over a medium-high heat, combine the remaining half of the blackberry mixture, sugar, golden syrup and salt in a medium saucepan. Stir together. Cook until the mixture reaches 240°F (115°C). Remove from the heat.

4. Set the stand mixer to slow. Slowly pour the sugar mixture into the stand mixer while running. Turn the mixer to high and mix for 10 to 15 minutes, or until it thickens. Near the end, add the vanilla extract.

note: If you notice the mixture has lightened too much, feel free to add additional purple food colouring.

5. Prepare the roasting tin by spraying with non-stick cooking spray and sprinkling with icing sugar.

6. Transfer the sugar mixture into the tin and spread evenly. Sprinkle the top with icing sugar. Allow the marshmallows to rest, uncovered, overnight. Use an oiled knife to cut the marshmallows to your desired size. The marshmallows can be stored in an airtight container for up to 2 weeks.

7. To serve, use yellow candy melts to shape an X matching Drifloon's marking. Serve each marshmallow portion with an X and a blob of whipped cream.

Munchlax
Custard Bao

All Munchlax thinks about is eating a vast amount of food. I bet it could even eat all ten bao from this recipe! But be careful! You'll have a serious stomach ache if you try the same. It would be best to share them!

Difficulty: ● ● ● ●
Prep Time: 3 hours
Rest Time: 12 hours
Cook Time: 45 minutes
Yield: 10 bao

Equipment: 2 large bowls, small bowl, whisk, sieve, medium saucepan, stand mixer with dough hook attachment, rolling pin, baking paper, large saucepan with steamer basket

note: It is very important that the milk is no warmer than 110°F (40°C) because if it is any warmer, it will kill the yeast and not allow the dough to rise. You can use a meat thermometer to check the temperature.

Custard Filling

4 egg yolks

½ vanilla pod, seeds scraped and pod discarded

½ cup (100 grams) sugar

1¾ cups (420 millilitres) whole milk

5 tablespoons plain flour

2 tablespoons cornflour

½ teaspoon rock salt

2 ounces (55 grams) unsalted butter, melted and cooled

1 teaspoon vanilla extract

White Dough

2 teaspoons active dry yeast

1 cup (240 millilitres) warm whole milk

2½ cups (400 grams) plain flour

½ cup (70 grams) cornflour

1½ teaspoons baking powder

¼ cup (50 grams) sugar

2 teaspoons rock salt

1 ounce (30 grams) unsalted butter, room temperature

Blue Dough

½ teaspoon active dry yeast

¼ cup (60 millilitres) warm whole milk

½ cup plus 2 tablespoons (100 grams) plain flour

2 tablespoons cornflour

⅓ teaspoon baking powder

1 tablespoon sugar

½ teaspoon rock salt

½ tablespoon unsalted butter, room temperature

Blue and black food colouring

To make the custard filling:

1. Put the egg yolks, vanilla pod seeds and sugar in a large bowl. Whisk together until completely combined. Add the milk and whisk until it is mixed in. Put the flour, cornflour and salt in a small bowl. Add the butter and flour mixture to the bowl with the egg yolks. Whisk together until well combined.

2. Place a sieve over a medium saucepan. Pass the mixture through the sieve. Make sure to press everything through if it has clumped up. Whisk the mixture in the saucepan over a medium heat until the mixture thickens into a thick paste, about 15 to 25 minutes. Once thickened, remove from the heat and whisk in the vanilla extract.

3. Transfer to an airtight container and allow to cool completely. Place a piece of cling film directly over it, cover and allow to rest in the refrigerator overnight, or at least 12 hours.

4. After it has rested, split the thickened custard into ten portions. Take each portion and roll into a ball in your hands. Return to the container, cover and place back in the refrigerator until needed.

To make the white dough:

1. Combine the yeast and milk. Allow to rest for 5 minutes, or until the yeast becomes active. Combine the flour, cornflour, baking powder, sugar and salt in the bowl of a stand mixer. Slowly mix in the liquid with the flour at a low speed. Blend until it all comes together.

2. Increase the speed to medium and allow to lightly knead. While the dough begins to knead, add the butter slowly. Knead the dough for 5 minutes. If the dough is too sticky, add 1 tablespoon of flour at a time. If it is too dry, add 1 tablespoon of milk at a time. Transfer to an oiled bowl, cover and let rest for 2 hours, or until it has doubled in size.

continued on the next page

To make the blue dough:

Repeat steps 1 and 2 of the white dough directions with one minor difference. Add the blue food colouring to the yeast and milk mixture. You may need several drops for a vibrant colour, depending on the strength of your food colouring.

To combine and bake:

1. Punch down the white dough and roll out to remove the air pockets. Set aside about 2 tablespoons of dough for the eyes and teeth. Split into ten equal portions. Take each portion and form into a smooth ball. Cover with a kitchen towel and let rest for 15 minutes.

2. Take a portion and roll out to about 5 inches (120 millimetres) wide. When rolling, make sure the centre is thicker than the edges. Add one of the custard portions in the centre. Wet your finger and lightly wet the edge of the dough. Pleat the buns until sealed. Flip the pleat side down and gently roll with your hand to smooth it out slightly. Place on a piece of baking paper, pleat side down. Repeat with the remaining portions.

3. Take a quarter of the set-aside white dough and add a drop of black food colouring. Rub together until it is dyed black. This will be used for the pupils.

note: You can use disposable, food safe gloves to avoid dying your hands.

4. Take the blue dough and roll it out very thin. Cut into a circle and cut off the bottom fifth of the dough. Take one of the baos. Lightly wet the prepared blue dough and drape over the bao. Wrap it and press into the bottom to stick to the dough.

5. Take 1 tablespoon of the blue dough and shape into one of Munchlax's ears.

6. Lightly wet the bottom and attach it to the top of the bao. Repeat this step for the other ear.

7. Take a small portion of the set-aside white dough and shape into two eyes and two teeth. Wet and place them on the bao to mimic Munchlax's face. Take a small amount of the black dough and make it into pupils. Place the completed Munchlax bao in a steamer basket.

8. Repeat steps 5–7 with the remaining portions.

9. Let the prepared bao rest for 30 minutes. Heat a saucepan that the steamer basket can sit on with water over a high heat and bring to the boil. Once boiling, reduce the heat to medium and place the steamer basket on top. Allow to steam for 15 to 20 minutes, until cooked through.

10. Turn off the heat and let sit, covered, for 5 minutes before serving the buns. This will help to prevent them from shrinking.

Abomasnow
Vichyssoise

Abomasnow has a massive body covered in snow and can cause blizzards on its own. Luckily, a nearby Abomasnow causing a blizzard won't ruin our vichyssoise. It's a soup that's served cold!

Difficulty: ● ● ○ ○
Prep Time: 30 minutes
Rest Time: 12 hours
Cook Time: 30 minutes
Yield: 4 to 6 servings

Equipment: Large saucepan, blender, sieve

2 tablespoons coconut oil
10 ounces (285 grams) leeks
1½ pounds (675 grams) maris piper potatoes, peeled and quartered
4 cups (960 millilitres) vegetable stock
1 bay leaf
½ cup (120 millilitres) coconut cream
Rock salt
Ground white pepper
Fresh chives, finely chopped, for garnishing

1. Put the coconut oil in a large saucepan and place over a medium-high heat. Allow the coconut oil to melt then add the leeks. Cook until the leeks are completely softened, about 8 minutes.

2. Add the potatoes and toss to mix. Add the vegetable stock and bay leaf. Bring to the boil. Reduce to a medium-low and simmer until the potatoes are tender, about 30 minutes.

3. Remove the bay leaf. Transfer everything else to a blender and blend until smooth. Pour through a sieve into an airtight container. Add the coconut cream and mix together. Season with salt and pepper to your liking. Allow to cool completely, cover and place in the refrigerator for at least 1 hour before serving. Serve in a bowl with chopped chives on top.

Weavile
Ice Lollies

Just like how Weavile works in a team, you'll want some friends to finish all these ice lollies. Otherwise, you'll get brain freeze!

Difficulty: ● ○ ○ ○
Prep Time: 30 minutes
Rest Time: 12 hours
Yield: 6 ice lollies

Equipment: Blender, ice lolly moulds

Raspberry Layer
3½ ounces (100 grams) frozen raspberries
¾ cup (180 millilitres) coconut milk
1 tablespoon sugar
½ teaspoon vanilla extract

Black Sesame Layer
⅓ cup (40 grams) black sesame seeds
½ cup (90 grams) chopped dark chocolate
1 cup (240 millilitres) coconut milk
¼ cup (50 grams) sugar
½ teaspoon almond extract
½ teaspoon rock salt

To make the raspberry layer:
1. Place all the ingredients in a blender and blend until smooth.

2. Transfer the mixture into the ice lolly moulds and fill each a third of the way up. Place in the freezer (without the sticks) for 30 minutes.

To make the black sesame layer:
1. Place the sesame seeds in a blender and blend until smooth. Scrape the side of the blender a few times while blending to make sure most of the seeds are blended.

2. Add the dark chocolate, coconut milk, sugar, almond extract and salt. Blend until completely smooth and well combined.

3. Transfer the mixture into the ice lolly moulds on top of the raspberry layer. Put in the ice lolly sticks, cover and place in the freezer overnight, at least 12 hours.

Froslass
Blackberry Ice Cream

Froslass loves frozen food, but we won't be adding any of that to this frozen dessert. Berries will do nicely to add some great flavour and a beautiful swirl.

Difficulty: ● ● ○ ○
Prep Time: 30 minutes
Rest Time: 12 hours
Cook Time: 30 minutes
Yield: 6 to 8 servings

Equipment: Medium saucepan, sieve, large bowl, stand mixer with whisk attachment

Blackberry Sauce
14 ounces (395 grams) fresh blackberries
2 tablespoons sugar
1 teaspoon rock salt
1 lemon, zested and juiced

Vanilla Ice Cream
14 ounces (395 grams) sweetened
    condensed milk
1 vanilla pod, seeds scraped and
    pod discarded
1 tablespoon vanilla extract
1 pinch rock salt
2 cups (480 millilitres) double cream
Blackberry sauce

To make the blackberry sauce:

1. Combine all the ingredients in a medium saucepan. Place over a medium-high and bring to the boil. Smash the blackberries. Reduce the heat and simmer for 20 minutes.

2. Remove from the heat and strain through a sieve into an airtight container. Once cooled, cover and store in the refrigerator for at least 12 hours and up to 2 weeks.

note: You can skip the step of straining through a sieve if you would like chunks of the fruit left in the ice cream. Either way will be delicious.

To make the vanilla ice cream:

1. Combine the sweetened condensed milk, vanilla pod seeds, vanilla extract and salt in a large bowl. Whisk together until well combined.

2. Place the double cream in the bowl of a stand mixer. Mix until the whipped cream forms medium peaks, abut 2 to 3 minutes. Transfer to the bowl with everything else. Carefully fold in the whipped cream until it is well combined.

3. Transfer to an airtight container, placing a third of the vanilla ice cream mixture in it. Pour half of the blackberry sauce and swirl it slightly into the vanilla mixture. Add another third of the vanilla mixture. Add the remaining blackberry sauce and top with the remaining vanilla mixture. Swirl slightly once more. Cover and place in the freezer for at least 5 hours before serving.

Unova Region

Pansage, Pansear
 and Panpour

Musharna

Swadloon

Darumaka

Crustle

Stunfisk

Pansage, Pansear and Panpour
Roasted Cauliflower

Pansear, Pansage and Panpour have their own strengths and weaknesses, but they love to be helpful to others. Why not help yourself to some tasty dips inspired by their unique attitudes?

Difficulty: ●○○○
Prep Time: 45 minutes
Cook Time: 20 minutes
Yield: 4 servings

Equipment: Large bowl, large baking sheet, tin foil, airtight containers, food processor

Roasted Cauliflower
2 cauliflowers, cut into large portions
¼ cup (60 millilitres) olive oil
1 teaspoon garlic powder
Non-stick cooking spray for greasing
Rock salt
Ground black pepper

Buffalo Sauce
¼ cup (60 millilitres) hot sauce
1 tablespoon gochujang
½ tablespoon maple syrup
2 ounces (55 grams) unsalted butter, melted
1 tablespoon (15 millilitres) rice vinegar
½ teaspoon cayenne pepper

Blue Cheese Dipping Sauce
3 ounces (85 grams) blue cheese, crumbled
¼ cup (60 grams) mayonnaise
3 tablespoons soured cream
3 tablespoons buttermilk
1 teaspoon lemon juice
1 drop of light blue food colouring
Rock salt
Ground black pepper

Green Chutney
Small bunch fresh coriander
1 serrano chilli, stemmed
3 garlic cloves
One ½-inch (12-millimetre) piece fresh ginger
1 teaspoon sugar
Rock salt
1 lime, juiced
2 tablespoons water
1 tablespoon yoghurt

To make the roasted cauliflower:
1. Preheat oven to 425°F (220°C). Place the cauliflower portions, olive oil and garlic powder in a large bowl. Toss until combined.

2. Prepare a large baking sheet with tin foil and spray with non-stick cooking spray. Transfer the cauliflower to the prepared baking sheet. Season generously with salt and pepper.

3. Place in the oven and bake for 15 minutes. Toss and bake for another 10 minutes, until golden and tender.

To make the buffalo sauce:
Combine all the ingredients. The buffalo sauce can be stored in an airtight container for up to 1 week.

To make the green chutney:
Place all the ingredients in a food processor and pulse until smooth. If the mixture is too thick, add a small amount of water at a time to loosen it. The chutney can be stored in an airtight container in the refrigerator for up to 1 week.

To make the blue cheese dipping sauce:
Combine all the ingredients. Season with salt and pepper. The dipping sauce can be stored in an airtight container in the refrigerator for up to 1 week.

Musharna
Strawberry Taro Slush

This strawberry and taro slush has its own beautiful pink swirls, reminiscent of the dark mist that emanates from a Musharna. It's sure to bring joy to even those who are grumpy.

Difficulty: ● ● ○ ○
Prep Time: 30 minutes
Yield: 2 drinks

Equipment: Stand mixer with whisk attachment, blender

Strawberry Whipped Cream

¾ cup (180 millilitres) double cream

2 tablespoons icing sugar

2½ tablespoons strawberry powder

2 drops pink food colouring

Taro Layer

2½ cups (600 millilitres) cold green tea

⅓ cup (60 grams) taro powder

½ cup (120 millilitres) coconut milk

2 tablespoons sweetened condensed milk

10 ice cubes

To make the strawberry whipped cream:

Place all the ingredients in the bowl of a stand mixer. Mix on a medium-high speed until the whipped cream forms stiff peaks, about 3 to 5 minutes. Transfer to a piping bag and store in the refrigerator until needed.

To make the taro layer:

1. Combine the green tea, taro powder, coconut milk and sweetened condensed milk in a blender. Blend until combined.

2. Add the ice cubes and blend until crushed. Pour into two glasses and top with the whipped cream.

Swadloon
Tofu Lettuce Wraps

Try to think of a Swadloon, wrapping itself up with leaves to protect itself from the cold, when you're eating these tofu lettuce wraps. You could even eat them while wrapped up in a blanket – but try not to make a mess!

Difficulty: ● ○ ○ ○
Prep Time: 30 minutes
Rest Time: 4 hours
Cook Time: 30 minutes
Yield: 2 to 3 servings

Equipment: Airtight container, chopping board, knife, peeler, grater, small bowl, large non-stick pan

Pickled Carrots and Daikon
½ cup (120 millilitres) rice vinegar
2 cups (480 millilitres) warm water
¼ cup (50 grams) sugar
2 tablespoons rock salt
2 carrots, julienned
1 small daikon radish, julienned

Lettuce Wraps
14 ounces (395 grams) firm tofu
¼ cup (60 millilitres) soy sauce
2 tablespoons hoisin sauce
1 tablespoon rice vinegar
2 teaspoons honey
1 teaspoon sesame oil
1 teaspoon ground turmeric
½ teaspoon ground ginger
½ teaspoon Chinese five-spice powder
2 teaspoons rapeseed oil
8 shiitake mushrooms, stemmed and chopped
8 ounces (225 grams) water chestnuts, chopped
6 garlic cloves, crushed
1 tablespoon grated fresh ginger
2 spring onions, chopped
1 head lettuce

To make the pickled carrots and daikon:
1. Combine the rice vinegar, warm water, sugar and salt in a large airtight container. Put the carrots and daikon radish into the container. If the carrots and daikon are not covered, add additional rice vinegar.

2. Cover and place in the refrigerator for at least 4 hours. The longer they are left to pickle, the more flavourful the carrots and daikon will become. The pickled carrots and daikon can be stored in the refrigerator for about 2 weeks.

To make the lettuce wraps:
1. Wrap the tofu in a paper towel. Place between two plates and top with a heavy object. Allow to rest for 5 minutes to remove excess liquid.

2. Combine the soy sauce, hoisin sauce, rice vinegar, honey, sesame oil, turmeric, ground ginger and Chinese five-spice powder in a small bowl. Set aside.

3. Heat a large non-stick pan with 1 teaspoon of rapeseed oil over a medium-high heat. Add the tofu and cook until all sides have turned golden brown, about 5 minutes. Transfer to a plate.

4. Add the remaining teaspoon of rapeseed oil and add the shiitake mushrooms and water chestnuts. Allow to cook until the mushrooms have softened, about 3 minutes. Toss in the garlic, fresh ginger and spring onions and cook for another 2 minutes, until the garlic becomes aromatic.

5. Add the tofu and the sauce mixture. Mix together to fully coat the tofu. Cook until the liquid has reduced by half, about 5 to 8 minutes. Remove from the heat and transfer to a bowl to serve.

6. To make a portion, take a piece of lettuce and top with the pickled vegetables and tofu.

Darumaka
Tomato Soup

Enjoy this soup when it's nice and hot, and you'll have a warm belly, just like Darumaka. But if you eat too much and get too full, you may fall asleep like Darumaka as well!

Difficulty: ● ● ○ ○
Prep Time: 30 minutes
Cook Time: 1½ hours
Yield: 4 servings

Equipment: Knife, chopping board, large bowl, large baking sheet, baking paper, medium saucepan, blender

Cheddar Croutons

1 baguette, cut into 1-inch (25 millimetre) cubes
½ cup (120 millilitres) olive oil
1 teaspoon garlic powder
½ teaspoon rock salt
5 ounces (140 grams) cheddar cheese, finely grated

Tomato Soup

3 tablespoons olive oil, plus more for greasing
Rock salt
Ground black pepper
3 pounds (1⅓ kilograms) tomatoes, quartered
18 garlic cloves, chopped
½ teaspoon red pepper flakes
1 tablespoon onion powder
2 cups (480 millilitres) vegetable stock

To make the cheddar croutons:

1. Preheat the oven to 350°F (175°C). Put the baguette pieces, olive oil, garlic powder and salt in a large bowl and toss until combined. Transfer to a large baking sheet, lined with baking paper, in a single layer. Sprinkle the cheddar cheese on top of the pieces of bread.

2. Bake for 10 minutes. Toss, then bake for another 5 to 10 minutes, or until they are golden brown. Allow to cool completely.

3. The croutons can be stored in an airtight container at room temperature for up to 1 week.

To make the tomato soup:

1. Preheat oven to 400°F (205°C). In a large bowl, combine the olive oil, salt and pepper. Add the tomatoes and toss to coat. Place the tomatoes on a large baking sheet and put in the oven to roast for 45 minutes, until tender and slightly charred.

2. Heat a medium saucepan with olive oil over a medium heat. Add the garlic. Cook until the garlic has turned golden brown, about 8 to 10 minutes. Add the red pepper flakes and onion powder. Cook for another 3 minutes, or until fragrant.

3. Add the roasted tomatoes and vegetable stock to the saucepan. Bring to the boil. Carefully transfer to a blender and blend until smooth. Return the mixture to the saucepan and heat back up.

4. Divide into four serving bowls and serve with croutons.

note: Serve the croutons on the side and place a few of them on top of the soup. Allow them to soften and absorb the soup.

Crustle
Parfaits

These parfaits are modelled after the boulders that Crustle carry around with them. The layering is up to you, so make sure to personalise it to your liking! But be sure to eat your parfait, not wear it.

Difficulty: ● ● ○ ○
Prep Time: 1 hour
Rest Time: 4 hours
Cook Time: 30 minutes
Yield: 4 parfaits, plus extra cookies

Equipment: Small bowl, stand mixer with paddle attachment, large baking sheet, baking paper, spatula, medium bowl, medium saucepan, whisk

Peanut Butter Biscuits

1¼ cups (200 grams) plain flour
1 teaspoon baking powder
½ teaspoon rock salt
1 cup (360 grams) smooth peanut butter
2 ounces (110 grams) unsalted butter, room temperature
2 tablespoons honey
⅓ cup (65 grams) light brown sugar
⅓ cup (75 grams) sugar
1 egg, room temperature
5 ounces (140 grams) peanut butter chips

Chocolate Biscuits

1½ cups (240 grams) plain flour
¼ cup (30 grams) dark chocolate powder
1 teaspoon baking powder
½ teaspoon rock salt
2 ounces (110 grams) unsalted butter, room temperature
⅓ cup (65 grams) sugar
⅓ cup (65 grams) light brown sugar
1 teaspoon vanilla extract
1 egg, room temperature
5 ounces (140 grams) dark chocolate chips

Chocolate Pudding

2 egg yolks
½ cup (100 grams) sugar, divided
2 tablespoons cornflour
2 cups (480 millilitres) milk
1 tablespoon cocoa powder
¼ teaspoon rock salt
5 ounces (140 grams) milk chocolate, melted
1 tablespoon vanilla extract
1 ounce (30 grams) unsalted butter, divided

To make the peanut butter biscuits:

1. Preheat the oven to 350°F (175°C). Combine the flour, baking powder and salt in a small bowl. Set aside. Place the peanut butter, butter and honey in the bowl of a stand mixer. Mix until smooth.

2. Add both sugars and mix until smooth. Add the egg and mix until just combined. Add the flour mixture and whip together until it just comes together. Fold in the peanut butter chips.

3. Prepare a large baking sheet with baking paper. Take about 1 tablespoon of the dough at a time, place on the baking sheet, and press down into a biscuit shape. Place in the oven to bake for 10 to 13 minutes, or until golden brown.

To make the chocolate biscuits:

1. Preheat the oven to 350°F (175°C). Combine the flour, dark chocolate powder, baking powder and salt in a small bowl. Set aside. Place the butter in the bowl of a stand mixer. Mix until smooth.

2. Add the sugar and mix until smooth. Add the vanilla extract and egg and mix until just combined. Add the flour mixture and whip together until it just comes together. Fold in the dark chocolate chips.

3. Prepare a large baking sheet with baking paper. Take about 1 tablespoon of the dough at a time, place on the baking sheet and press down into a biscuit shape. Place in the oven to bake for 14 to 16 minutes, or until the centre is set and firm.

To make the chocolate pudding:

1. Combine the egg yolks, half the sugar and cornflour in a medium bowl. Whisk in a quarter of the milk and set the bowl aside. Whisk together the remaining milk and sugar, the cocoa powder and salt in a medium saucepan. Place over a medium-high heat. Get the mixture hot enough to right before it starts to boil. Reduce the heat to low.

2. Scoop out a third of the cocoa mixture and place it in the bowl with the egg yolks. Whisk the contents together! Add another third of cocoa mixture to the bowl while still whisking. Repeat this one last time.

3. Slowly add the mixture into the saucepan. Whisk everything together until it thickens. This step should take about 5 to 10 minutes.

4. Once the base has thickened, remove it from the heat. Stir in the melted chocolate. Add the vanilla extract and butter. Place the pudding into an airtight container and allow to cool to room temperature. Place in the refrigerator for 4 hours before setting up the parfait.

5. To assemble a parfait, take a large bowl or cup and crumble a layer of the chocolate biscuits on the bottom. Press it down into a smooth layer. Top with a portion of the pudding. Add a layer of crumbled peanut butter biscuits. Top again with another portion of pudding. Top with either a layer of crumbed chocolate biscuits or peanut butter biscuits.

Stunfisk
Flatbreads

No other food could represent the flatness of a Stunfisk more than a flatbread. And with different recipes, your flatbread can look like whichever Stunfisk is your favourite!

Difficulty: ● ● ○ ○
Prep Time: 1 hour
Rest Time: 2 hours
Cook Time: 30 minutes
Yield: 10 flatbreads

Equipment: Food processor, stand mixer with dough hook attachment, medium bowl, rolling pin, large cast-iron frying pan

Black Sesame Hummus

16 ounces (440 grams) canned chickpeas, drained and rinsed
2 tablespoons shiro miso
$\frac{1}{3}$ cup (40 grams) black sesame seeds
1 tablespoon honey
2 garlic cloves
2 tablespoons lemon juice
2 tablespoons water
1 tablespoon olive oil

Dessert Flatbread

¾ cup (180 millilitres) warm water
½ teaspoon vanilla extract
1 tablespoon olive oil
2 tablespoons sugar
1 teaspoon active dry yeast
2 cups (320 grams) plain flour
1 teaspoon ground cardamom
½ teaspoon rock salt
Chocolate hazelnut spread for topping
Sliced banana for topping

Savoury Flatbread

¼ cup (30 grams) black sesame seeds
1 tablespoon honey
¾ cup (180 millilitres) warm water
1 tablespoon olive oil
2 tablespoons sugar
1 teaspoon active dry yeast
2 cups (320 grams) plain flour
1 teaspoon rock salt
Black sesame hummus for topping
Fresh mozzarella for topping
Arugula for topping
Mini tomatoes for topping
Balsamic vinegar for topping

To make the black sesame hummus:

Place all the ingredients in a food processor. Pulse until the mixture is smooth. If the mixture is too thick to mix, add 1 teaspoon of water at a time. Transfer to an airtight container and store in the refrigerator. The hummus can be stored for up to 1 week.

To make the dessert flatbread:

1. Combine the water, vanilla extract, olive oil, sugar and yeast in the bowl of a stand mixer. Whisk together and set aside for 10 minutes to allow the yeast to get frothy. Combine the plain flour, cardamom and salt in a medium bowl.

2. Add a third of the flour mixture to the stand mixer bowl. Mix at low speed until the dough just starts to come together. Add another third of the flour mixture and keep mixing. Repeat with the last third and mix until the dough is smooth and tacky. If the dough is too sticky, add 1 tablespoon of plain flour until it becomes tacky. Knead the dough for 5 minutes.

3. Transfer the dough ball into an oiled bowl and toss the dough in the oil until all sides are covered. Cover the bowl with cling film and let the dough rest until it has doubled in size, about 2 hours.

4. Lightly flour a worktop and place the dough on the counter. Lightly pat and divide the dough into five equal pieces. Tuck in the sides and form each of the pieces into a ball. Cover the dough with a towel and let it rest for 30 minutes.

5. Working on a lightly floured worktop, take a ball and pat down with your hands. With a rolling pin, roll out into the shape of Stunfisk, about 9 inches (230 millimetres) long.

6. Place a large skillet over a medium-high heat. Make sure the skillet is hot. Take a rolled-out piece of dough and flip it onto the skillet. Cook until the disk begins to turn golden brown, about 2 to 3 minutes. Flip and repeat on the other side, about 2 minutes. Place the cooked flatbread on a plate and cover with a kitchen towel. Repeat with the remaining disks. To store, allow the flatbreads to cool completely and place them in a resealable bag. They will remain fresh for up to 4 days.

7. To assemble, while the flatbread is warm, spread a generous amount of chocolate hazelnut spread and top with the sliced bananas.

continued on the next page

To make the savoury flatbread:

1. Place the black sesame seeds in a food processor and pulse until smooth. Add the honey until it forms a smooth paste.

2. Combine the black sesame seeds, water, olive oil, sugar and yeast in the bowl of a stand mixer. Whisk together and set aside for 10 minutes to allow the yeast to get frothy. Combine the plain flour and salt in a medium bowl.

3. Add a third of the flour mixture to the stand mixer bowl. Mix at a low speed until the dough just starts to come together. Add another third of the flour mixture and keep mixing. Repeat with the last third and mix until the dough is smooth and tacky. If the dough is too sticky, add 1 tablespoon of plain flour until it becomes tacky. Knead the dough for 5 minutes.

4. Transfer the dough ball into an oiled bowl and toss the dough in the oil until all sides are covered. Cover the bowl with cling film and let the dough rest until it has doubled in size, about 2 hours.

5. Lightly flour a worktop and place the dough on the counter. Lightly pat and divide the dough into five equal pieces. Tuck in the sides and form each of the pieces into a ball. Cover the dough with a towel and let it rest for 30 minutes.

6. Working on a lightly floured worktop, take a ball and pat down with your hands. With a rolling pin, roll out into the shape of Stunfisk, about 9 inches (230 millimetres) long.

7. Place a skillet over a medium-high heat. Make sure the skillet is hot. Take a rolled-out piece of dough and flip it onto the skillet. Cook until the disk begins to turn golden brown, about 2 to 3 minutes. Flip and repeat on the other side, about 2 minutes. Place the cooked flatbread on a plate and cover with a kitchen towel. Repeat with the remaining disks. To store, allow the flatbreads to cool completely and place them in a resealable bag. They will remain fresh for up to 4 days.

8. To assemble, while the flatbread is warm, spread a generous amount of the black sesame hummus. Top with fresh mozzarella, arugula, mini tomatoes and balsamic vinegar.

Kalos Region

Pyroar
Gogoat
Pancham
Sylveon
Dedenne
Sliggoo

Pyroar
Bruschetta

Pyroar's fire breath can get to over 10,000°F, but we won't need nearly that much heat to prepare these bruschetta. A typical kitchen oven will do the job nicely.

Difficulty: ● ○ ○ ○
Prep Time: 30 minutes
Cook Time: 1 hour
Yield: 15 to 20 bruschettas

Equipment: Knife, chopping board, large baking sheet, small non-stick pan, medium bowl

2 yellow bell peppers, halved and seeded
Rock salt
Ground black pepper
1 tablespoon olive oil, plus more for brushing
5 garlic cloves, crushed
12 ounces (340 grams) tomatoes, chopped
4 to 6 Calabrian chilli peppers
Fresh basil, thinly sliced
1 teaspoon balsamic vinegar
1 baguette, cut into medium slices

1. Heat the oven to 450°F (230°C). Place the bell peppers on a baking sheet, skin side up. Brush with olive oil and season with salt and pepper. Bake in the oven for 30 to 40 minutes, until they have softened and the skin has charred slightly. Remove the bell peppers from the oven and allow to cool.

2. Remove the skin and discard. Cut the bell peppers into thick slices and set aside. Reduce the oven to 400°F (205°C).

3. Place a small non-stick pan over a medium-high heat. Add half the olive oil and the garlic. Cook until the garlic is golden brown, about 3 to 5 minutes. Once cooked, place the cooked garlic in a medium bowl. Add the tomatoes, Calabrian chilli peppers, basil, the remaining olive oil and the balsamic vinegar. Season with salt and pepper.

4. Place the baguette slices on a large baking sheet and bake for 4 minutes. Flip and bake for another 4 minutes, or until crispy and golden. Once baked, take each of the baked slices and brush olive oil over them. Place a portion of the tomato mixture on top of each slice. Top with a piece of bell pepper.

Gogoat
Breakfast Burritos

Gogoats travel along mountain trails with their herds or their rider. If you've got plans to explore the outdoors, a hearty meal like these breakfast burritos is a great way to prepare for fun activities outside.

Difficulty: ● ● ○ ○
Prep Time: 30 minutes
Cook Time: 30 minutes
Yield: 4 servings

Equipment: Vegetable peeler, box grater, knife, chopping board, medium bowl, 2 medium non-stick pans

Hash Browns

1 large russet potato, peeled and shredded
1 tablespoon garlic powder
2 teaspoons onion powder
1 tablespoon olive oil
Rock salt
Ground black pepper

Burritos

2 teaspoons rapeseed oil
8 baby portobello mushrooms, sliced
6 ounces (170 grams) spinach
4 eggs
4 8-inch (20-centimetre) wholegrain tortillas
8 ounces (225 grams) refried beans, warmed up
1 avocado, sliced
Fresh coriander, chopped

To make the hash browns:

1. Combine the shredded potato, garlic powder and onion powder in a medium bowl. Heat a medium non-stick pan with olive oil over a medium-high heat. Add the shredded potato. Generously season with salt and pepper. Allow the potato to cook until the bottom has browned, about 5 to 8 minutes.

2. Carefully flip the potato. Season with salt and pepper again. Cook until the other side has browned completely, about 5 minutes. Split into four portions and set aside.

To make the burritos:

1. Heat a medium non-stick pan with 1 teaspoon rapeseed oil over a medium heat. Add the mushrooms and cook until golden brown, about 10 to 15 minutes. Remove from the pan and set aside. Add the spinach and cook until just wilted, about 1 minute.

2. Crack and scramble the eggs in a medium bowl. Heat a medium non-stick pan over a medium heat with the remaining rapeseed oil. Pour the scrambled egg into the pan and let it cook fully, about 2 to 3 minutes. Split into four portions and set aside.

3. Heat up the tortillas and prepare to assemble. Take a tortilla and add a layer of refried beans. Top with the mushrooms, scrambled eggs, hash browns, avocado slices and chopped coriander and carefully wrap. Heat a medium non-stick pan over a medium-high heat. Place the wrapped burrito, crease side down. Cook until golden brown, about 2 minutes. Flip and cook until golden brown again, about 2 minutes. Repeat with the remaining tortillas.

note: There are many vegetables that would work well in this burrito. Pick your favourite to make these your own!

Pancham
Rice Bowls

Pancham always seems to be glaring at others, but sometimes it forgets to keep up the tough exterior and smiles. Try your best Pancham impersonation and then decorate the bowl to look the same way.

Difficulty: ● ● ○ ○
Prep Time: 30 minutes
Rest Time: 10 minutes
Cook Time: 20 minutes
Yield: 4 servings

Equipment: Knife, chopping board, large non-stick pan, small bowl

Sauce
¼ cup (60 millilitres) water
1 teaspoon potato flour
2 tablespoons soy sauce
1 teaspoon white vinegar
1 teaspoon sesame oil
2 tablespoons maple syrup

Rice Bowl
16 ounces (450 grams) firm tofu
2 teaspoons rapeseed oil
6 shiitake mushrooms, sliced
8 ounces (225 grams) green beans
1 aubergine, cut into bite-size pieces
6 ounces (170 grams) tenderstem broccoli, cut into bite-size pieces
8 ounces (225 grams) beansprouts
Rock salt
Pepper
3 cups (420 grams) cooked rice
2 sheets nori
4 Thai basil leaves

To make the sauce:
Combine the ingredients in a small bowl and set aside.

To make the rice bowl:
1. Place the tofu between two plates and top with a heavy object. Allow this to rest for 10 minutes to remove excess liquid.

2. Heat a large non-stick pan with 1 teaspoon rapeseed oil over a medium-high heat. Add the tofu and cook until all sides have slightly browned, about 5 to 8 minutes. Transfer to a plate.

3. Add the remaining rapeseed oil and add the shiitake mushrooms, green beans, aubergine and tenderstem broccoli. Cook until the vegetables have softened, about 5 to 8 minutes. Add the tofu and toss to combine.

4. Add the sauce, toss to coat everything, and cook until the sauce has reduced and thickened, about 3 minutes. Add the beansprouts and cook for another 2 minutes. Season with salt and pepper. Remove from the heat and set aside to serve.

5. Prepare the cooked rice by shaping it like Pancham's face. Use nori pieces to add the details of Pancham's face. Finally, add a Thai basil leaf to mimic the small leaf in Pancham's mouth. Serve the portion of rice with the stir-fried vegetables.

Sylveon
Strawberry Shortcake

Sylveon is capable of stopping any conflict, releasing enmity-erasing waves and bringing peace to those around it. A bite of these minty strawberry shortcakes is a perfect substitute to help everyone relax.

Difficulty: ● ● ○ ○
Prep Time: 30 minutes
Rest Time: 1 hour
Cook Time: 30 minutes
Yield: 12 strawberry shortcakes

Equipment: Medium bowl, large baking sheet, baking paper, stand mixer with whisk attachment, small bowl, wire rack

Biscuits

3 cups (480 grams) plain flour
2 tablespoons sugar
1 tablespoon baking powder
2 teaspoons rock salt
8 ounces (225 grams) unsalted butter, cubed and chilled in the freezer for at least 20 minutes
1¼ cups (300 millilitres) buttermilk, chilled
1 ounce (30 grams) unsalted butter, melted
Coarse sugar for sprinkling

Mint Whipped Cream

1½ cups (360 millilitres) double cream
1 tablespoon icing sugar
½ teaspoon peppermint extract
1 pinch rock salt
3 drops light blue food colouring

Sweetened Strawberries

16 ounces (450 grams) fresh strawberries
2 tablespoons sugar

To make the biscuits:

1. Put the flour, sugar, baking powder and salt in a medium bowl. Add the cubed butter and combine with your hands until it resembles breadcrumbs. Place in the refrigerator and let rest for 15 minutes.

2. Remove from the refrigerator, add the buttermilk and stir until the dough barely comes together. Transfer to a floured worktop and work until the dough just comes together. Roll the dough into a 1-inch-tall rectangle. Fold the top third of the dough towards you. Next, fold the bottom third over the first fold. Reroll the dough again and repeat the fold. Reroll the dough once more. Cut the dough into 12 triangle pieces.

3. Preheat oven to 425°F (220°C). Place the pieces on a large baking sheet with baking paper. Place in the freezer for 20 minutes. Remove and brush each of the biscuits with melted butter and sprinkle on coarse sugar. Bake for 15 to 20 minutes, or until golden brown. Transfer to a wire rack and allow to cool.

To make the mint whipped cream:

1. Place the double cream, icing sugar, peppermint extract and salt in the bowl of a stand mixer. Mix on a medium-high speed until the whipped cream forms stiff peaks, about 3 to 5 minutes.

2. Split the whipped cream in half. Add the light blue food colouring to one half and fold in.

3. Store in the refrigerator until needed.

To make the sweetened strawberries:

Place the strawberries and sugar in a small bowl and allow to rest for 30 minutes.

For assembly:

1. Cut a biscuit in half and place the bottom piece on a plate. Top with the light blue whipped cream. Place a generous portion of strawberries on top.

2. Top with the white whipped cream and place the biscuit on top.

3. Decorate with melted pink chocolate (optional), additional whipped cream and strawberries.

Dedenne
Ramen

Dedenne can't generate much electricity on its own, but it always knows where to go to store up energy for its next Pokémon battle. A heaping bowl of ramen is a great source of energy for those on the go!

Difficulty: ● ● ● ○
Prep Time: 30 minutes
Rest Time: 24 hours
Cook Time: 40 minutes
Yield: 4 to 6 servings

Equipment: Medium saucepan, medium bowl, small non-stick pan, small bowl, large saucepan

Ajitsuke Tamago
4 eggs
½ cup (120 millilitres) soy sauce
¼ cup (50 grams) sugar
¼ cup (60 millilitres) water
2 tablespoons vegetarian oyster sauce

Curry Stock
¼ cup (40 grams) plain flour
1½ tablespoons garam masala
1½ tablespoons ground turmeric
1 teaspoon ground fennel seeds
1 teaspoon ground fenugreek seeds
½ teaspoon cinnamon
½ teaspoon cayenne pepper
2 ounces (55 grams) unsalted butter
3 tablespoons tomato paste
2 teaspoons tonkatsu sauce
1 tablespoon honey
1 tablespoon rapeseed oil
½ red onion, sliced
5 shiitake mushrooms, thinly sliced
5 cups (1200 millilitres) vegetable stock
2 golden potatoes, peeled and cut into bite-size pieces
2 carrots, peeled and cut into bite-size pieces
¼ cup (60 millilitres) soy sauce

For assembly, per serving
1 portion ramen noodles
2 pieces aburaage tofu, sliced
1 ajitsuke tamago, halved
1 spring onion, sliced
Nori for garnishing

To make the ajitsuke tamago:
1. Bring a medium saucepan of water to the boil. Gently place the eggs in the saucepan, cover and cook for 6½ minutes. Once cooked, immediately take the saucepan off the heat and place under cold running water. Move the contents to a medium bowl with ice cubes and water. Let rest for 5 minutes. Carefully remove the shells from the eggs.

2. Mix the soy sauce, sugar, water and vegetarian oyster sauce in a resealable bag. Add the eggs. Seal and make sure the eggs are fully covered. Place in the refrigerator and marinate for at least 24 hours. The eggs can be stored in the refrigerator for up to 3 days.

To make the curry stock:
1. Combine the flour, garam masala, turmeric, fennel, fenugreek, cinnamon and cayenne pepper in a small bowl. In a small non-stick pan, over a medium-high heat, melt the butter. Add the flour and spices to the melted butter.

2. Mix together until the flour has absorbed all the butter. Add the tomato paste, tonkatsu sauce and honey. Once combined, turn off the heat and set the roux aside.

3. Heat a large saucepan with rapeseed oil over a medium-high heat. Add the onions and shiitake mushrooms. Cook until softened, about 5 minutes.

4. Add the vegetable stock, potatoes and carrots. Bring to the boil and then reduce the heat to have the liquid at a simmer. Place the lid slightly ajar and simmer for 20 minutes.

5. Take a small portion of the roux and place it in a ladle. Place the ladle in the liquid of the saucepan and slowly mix in the roux. Repeat in small portions until all the roux is added to the saucepan. Add the soy sauce. Let simmer for 5 minutes.

To serve the ramen bowls:
Prepare a serving of ramen noodles and the stock with potatoes and carrots. Top with the aburaage, ajitsuke tamago, spring onions and nori.

note: If you want to shape this like Dedenne, cut the aburaage in the shape of Dedenne and place on the bowl. Make sure to leave a portion of the ramen noodles to represent the belly. It is also extremely helpful to pre-cut the nori into the shape of the whiskers and eyes ahead of time.

Sliggoo
Purple Cauliflower Soup

Sliggoo isn't very strong, but it's important to handle with great care. You'll want to take the same care carrying this cauliflower and potato soup, which is just the thing to satisfy your hunger.

Difficulty: ● ● ○ ○
Prep Time: 30 minutes
Cook Time: 1½ hours
Yield: 4 to 6 servings

Equipment: 2 large baking sheets, tin foil, 2 medium bowls, 2 medium saucepans, blender

Light Purple Soup
1 head purple cauliflower, cut into bite-size pieces
2 tablespoons olive oil
Rock salt
Ground black pepper
2 shallots, chopped
3 garlic cloves, crushed
1½ cups (360 millilitres) vegetable stock
½ cup (60 millilitres) coconut milk

Dark Purple Soup
Non-stick cooking spray for greasing
16 ounces (450 grams) purple sweet potato, peeled and cut into bite-size pieces
2 tablespoons olive oil
Rock salt
Ground black pepper
½ red onion, chopped
3 garlic cloves, crushed
2 cups (480 millilitres) vegetable stock
Fresh chives, finely chopped, for garnishing

To start the dark purple soup:
1. Preheat the oven to 375°F (190°C). Prepare 2 large baking sheets with tin foil and non-stick cooking spray.

2. Place the purple sweet potato in a medium bowl. Add half the olive oil and toss until coated.

3. Transfer to one of the baking sheets and generously season with salt and pepper. Place in the oven and cook for 45 to 60 minutes, until softened and cooked through.

To make the light purple soup:
1. When the sweet potatoes are about halfway through their cooking time, place the cauliflower in a medium bowl and toss with half the olive oil until coated.

2. Transfer to the other baking sheet and generously season with salt and pepper. Place in the oven and cook for 25 to 30 minutes, until golden, softened and cooked through.

3. Heat a medium saucepan with the remaining olive oil over a medium-high heat. Add the shallot and garlic and cook until softened, about 5 minutes. Add the cauliflower and toss to coat.

4. Add the vegetable stock and bring to the boil. Reduce the heat and simmer for 20 minutes. Remove from the heat and transfer to a blender.

5. Blend until smooth. Return to the saucepan and add the coconut milk. Heat until everything is warmed up.

To make the dark purple soup:

1. Heat a medium saucepan with the remaining olive oil over a medium-high heat. Add the red onion and garlic and cook until softened, about 3 minutes. Add the sweet potatoes and toss to coat.

2. Add the vegetable stock and bring to the boil. Reduce the heat and simmer for 20 minutes. Remove from the heat and transfer to a blender.

3. Blend until smooth. Return to the saucepan and heat until everything is warmed up.

For assembly:
1. To serve, pour a portion of each of the soups into a bowl and garnish with freshly chopped chives.

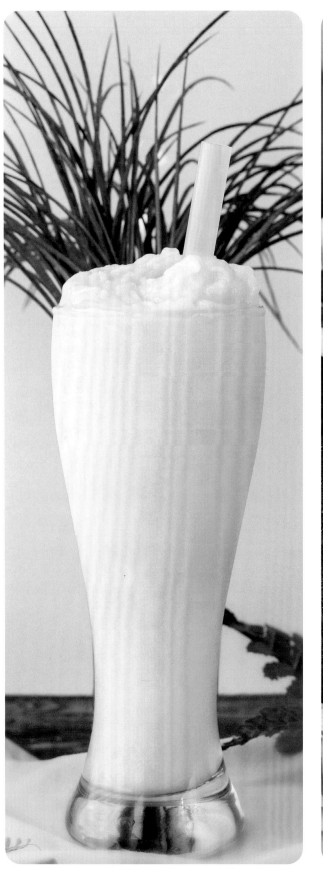

Alola Region

Incineroar

Mudbray

Bewear

Tsareena

Bruxish

Alolan Exeggutor

Incineroar
Aubergine Parmigiana Sandwiches

These deliciously spicy sandwiches have heat to rival Incineroar's flames. Show off your best fighting spirit after eating one!

Difficulty: ● ● ○ ○
Prep Time: 45 minutes
Rest Time: 15 minutes
Cook Time: 40 minutes
Yield: 3 sandwiches

Equipment: Medium saucepan, large deep-frying pan, large baking sheet, small bowl, medium bowl

Spicy Marinara
3 tablespoons olive oil
6 garlic cloves, crushed
½ onion, finely chopped
2 tablespoons tomato paste
1 tablespoon gochujang
1 teaspoon sweet paprika
2 teaspoons crushed red pepper flakes
1 tablespoon sugar
One 28-ounce (2x 400-gram) can whole tomatoes
Rock salt
Ground black pepper

Fried Aubergine
1 aubergine, thickly sliced
½ cup (80 grams) plain flour
1 teaspoon rock salt, plus more for salting the aubergine
1 teaspoon ground black pepper
1 teaspoon garlic powder
1 pinch cayenne
2 eggs
1 tablespoon milk
1 cup (70 grams) panko breadcrumbs
½ cup (70 grams) regular breadcrumbs
1 teaspoon dried oregano
1 teaspoon dried basil
Peanut oil for frying

Per Serving
1 ciabatta
2 whole black garlic cloves
2 ounces (55 grams) unsalted butter, room temperature
3 slices fried aubergine
Spicy marinara for topping
Fresh mozzarella for topping
Fresh basil for topping

To make the spicy marinara:

1. Heat a medium saucepan with olive oil over a medium-high heat. Add the garlic and onion. Cook until softened, about 5 minutes. Add the tomato paste and gochujang and allow to cook for another 2 minutes.

2. Add the paprika, red pepper flakes and sugar. Mix to combine. Take the whole tomatoes and crush them with your hands. Add them to the pan. Reduce the heat to a medium-low and simmer for 30 minutes. Season with salt and pepper. Set aside until you are ready to put the sandwiches together.

To make the aubergine:

1. Place the cut aubergine in a sieve and cover generously with salt. Place a plate on top and add some weight. Let it sit for 15 minutes. This step is done to remove some of the liquid in the aubergine. Do not skip it! Your aubergine will be soggy if you do.

2. Combine the flour, salt, pepper, garlic powder and cayenne on a plate. Combine the egg and milk in a medium bowl. Combine the panko, regular breadcrumbs, oregano and basil on another plate.

3. Take the aubergine and pat with a paper towel to remove the excess liquid. Take one of the aubergine slices and dip it in the flour mixture. Cover it well in flour. Dip it in the egg mixture. Cover it completely. Let any excess liquid drip off the aubergine and then place it in the breadcrumb mixture.

4. In a large deep-frying pan, add ½ inch of peanut oil and let the oil heat up to roughly 360°F (180°C). It is ready when you add a small piece of panko and the oil sizzles. Add the breaded aubergine and fry for 3 minutes per side, or until golden brown. Once cooked, transfer onto a plate with a paper towel to drain excess oil. Repeat until all the aubergine is cooked.

For assembly:

1. Preheat the grill. Slice the roll in half and place on a large baking sheet. Combine the black garlic and butter in a small bowl. Spread the inside of each of the rolls with the combined butter. Place under the grill and toast until the rolls have crisped up, about 2 minutes.

> **note:** This is more butter than you'll need for a single serving. This mixture can be stored in an airtight container for up to 1 week.

2. To assemble, place a small amount of spicy marinara on the bottom portion of the roll. Top with the fried aubergine, more sauce, fresh mozzarella and basil. Put on the roll top and serve.

Mudbray
Babka

Chocolate babka can be a messy meal to make, so be sure to clean up afterwards. You may want to feel like a Mudbray and get chocolate all over your hands, but you'll just make cleaning up that much harder.

Difficulty: ● ● ● ○
Prep Time: 1 hour
Rest Time: 2 hours
Cook Time: 20 minutes
Yield: 6 buns

Equipment: Stand mixer with dough hook attachment, knife, large bowl, medium saucepan, large baking sheet, baking paper

Dough
¾ cup (180 millilitres) milk, heated to 100°F (40°C)
1 teaspoon active dry yeast
3½ cups (560 grams) plain flour
½ teaspoon grated nutmeg
¼ cup (50 grams) sugar
1 teaspoon rock salt
2 eggs
1 teaspoon vanilla extract
3 ounces (85 grams) unsalted butter, room temperature

Filling
3 ounces (85 grams) unsalted butter
⅓ cup (60 grams) chopped dark chocolate
3 tablespoons cocoa powder
1 ounce (30 grams) almond butter
⅓ cup (45 grams) icing sugar
2 teaspoons rock salt

Syrup
3 tablespoons water
¼ cup (50 grams) sugar

To make the dough:
1. Combine the milk and yeast. Allow the yeast to bloom, about 5 minutes. Combine the flour, nutmeg, sugar and salt in the bowl of a stand mixer. Add the yeast mixture, eggs and vanilla extract. Mix until it just comes together.

2. While the dough begins to knead, add the butter 1 tablespoon at a time. Knead the dough for 5 minutes. If the dough is too sticky, add 1 tablespoon of flour at a time. If it is too dry, add 1 tablespoon of milk at a time. Transfer to an oiled bowl, cover and let rest for 1 hour, or until it has doubled in size.

To make the filling:
1. Place the butter in a medium saucepan over a medium heat. Allow the butter to melt. Once melted, add the remaining ingredients for the filling and mix together until the chocolate is melted. Remove from the heat and set aside.

2. Transfer the dough to a lightly floured worktop and punch down. Lightly knead for 1 minute. Divide into six equal portions and cover with a kitchen towel.

3. Take one of the portions and roll out into an 8-by-5-inch (200-by-125-millimetre) rectangle. Take a generous portion of the filling and spread it on the dough, leaving a ¼-inch (6-millimetre) border. Tightly roll the dough and pinch the seam to seal.

4. Cut the roll in half lengthwise, but not all the way through, leaving one end connected on the bottom. Turn the cut ends upwards. Tightly braid the two pieces together and pinch the end of the braid together. Shape the braided log into a tight circle and knot the two ends closed. Place on a large baking sheet with baking paper, leaving 3 inches (75 millimetres) in between each bun. Repeat steps 3 and 4 with the remaining portions.

5. Once all the buns are set, cover the tray with a kitchen towel and allow to rest for 1 hour, or until risen.

To make the syrup:
1. Combine the water and sugar in a medium saucepan over a medium-high heat. Mix together. Once the sugar dissolves, reduce the heat to a medium-low and simmer for 10 minutes. Remove from the heat and set aside.

2. Preheat the oven to 350°F (175°C). Brush each of the buns with the syrup. Place in the oven and bake for 20 minutes, or until golden brown.

Bewear
Raspberry Chocolate Cupcakes

Though sharing a hug with friends is a nice gesture, Bewear's hugs are too powerful. Perhaps it would like to share this tasty cupcake instead.

Difficulty: ● ● ● ○
Prep Time: 1 hour
Cook Time: 20 minutes
Yield: 14 to 15 cupcakes

Equipment: Stand mixer with paddle attachment, small bowl, medium bowl, whisk, muffin tray

Dark Chocolate Cupcakes

¼ cup (60 millilitres) hot water
2 tablespoons raspberry jam
2 tablespoons dark cocoa powder
1¼ cups (200 grams) plain flour
1 teaspoon baking powder
½ teaspoon rock salt
½ cup (110 grams) unsalted butter, room
    temperature
4 ounces (110 grams) sugar
¼ cup (50 grams) brown sugar
3 ounces (85 grams) dark chocolate, melted and
    cooled
2 eggs
1 teaspoon vanilla extract
½ cup (120 grams) soured cream
¼ cup (60 millilitres) double cream

Frosting

4 ounces (110 grams) cream cheese, room
    temperature
2 ounces (55 grams) unsalted butter, room
    temperature
1 teaspoon vanilla extract
3 drops pink food colouring
⅓ cup (120 grams) raspberry jam
3 cups (420 grams) icing sugar

To make the dark chocolate cupcakes:

1. Preheat the oven to 350°F (175°C). Combine the hot water, raspberry jam and cocoa powder in a small bowl. Whisk together until smooth. Combine the flour, baking powder and rock salt in a medium bowl.

2. Place the butter in the bowl of a stand mixer and mix until creamed and smooth. Add the sugars and melted dark chocolate. Mix until smooth. Add and mix in the eggs one at a time. Add the vanilla extract and cocoa powder mixture and mix until combined.

3. Mix in a third of the flour mixture. Follow that with half of the soured cream. Add another third of the flour mixture and then the remaining soured cream and the double cream. Finally, mix in the last of the flour.

4. Take your muffin tray and fill them three quarters of the way up with the batter. Bake for 15 to 20 minutes, or until they pass the cocktail stick test. Allow the cupcakes to cool completely before decorating.

To make the frosting:

1. Place the cream cheese and butter in the bowl of a stand mixer and mix. Add the vanilla extract, pink food colouring and raspberry jam.

2. Once it is well mixed, begin to slowly add the icing sugar. Add until the cream cheese frosting has thickened enough to pipe. Transfer to a piping bag with a frosting tip of your choice. Frost each of the cupcakes.

Tsareena
Roast Beetroot Salad

If you want to grow up strong like Tsareena, you'll need a balanced diet with plenty of vegetables. If you had powerful kicks just like Tsareena, think of all the sports and other activities in which you could excel.

Difficulty: ● ○ ○ ○
Prep Time: 45 minutes
Cook Time: 1 hour
Yield: 4 to 6 servings

Equipment: Medium baking tray, tin foil, small bowl, large bowl, chopping board, knife

Roasted Beetroot

3 red beetroots, leaves and stems removed
1 tablespoon olive oil
Rock salt
Ground black pepper

Orange Shallot Vinaigrette

1 small shallot, finely chopped
2 garlic cloves, crushed
¼ cup (60 millilitres) orange juice
1 orange, zested
1 tablespoon apple cider vinegar
1 tablespoon honey
1 tablespoon Dijon mustard
⅓ cup (80 millilitres) olive oil
Rock salt
Ground black pepper

Salad

4 ounces (110 grams) spinach
8 ounces (225 grams) rocket
4 ounces (110 grams) goat's cheese, crumbled
½ red onion, thinly sliced
4 ounces (110 grams) walnuts, coarsely chopped

To make the roasted beetroots:

1. Preheat the oven to 400°F (205°C). Rub the beetroots with olive oil. Generously season with salt and pepper. Take one of the beetroots, place it on a sheet of tin foil and wrap it shut. Repeat with the remaining beetroots.

2. Place the foil-wrapped beetroots on a medium baking tray. Transfer to the oven and roast for 45 to 60 minutes, until tender.

3. Allow the beetroots to cool before peeling and discarding the skin. Thinly slice the beetroots into ¼-inch (6-millimetre) thick bite-size pieces. The sliced beetroots can be stored in an airtight container in the refrigerator for up to 1 week.

To make the orange shallot vinaigrette:

1. Combine the shallots, garlic, orange juice, orange zest, apple cider vinegar, honey and Dijon mustard in a small bowl. Let sit for 20 minutes. Whisk in the olive oil and season with salt and pepper to your liking.

2. The vinaigrette can be stored in an airtight container in the refrigerator for up to 1 week. The oil and acid will separate after sitting for a while, so make sure to shake vigorously before serving.

To make the salad:

Combine the spinach and rocket in a large bowl and toss until well mixed. Transfer an equal portion to six salad bowls. Top each with roasted beetroots, goat cheese, red onion and walnuts. Serve with the orange shallot vinaigrette.

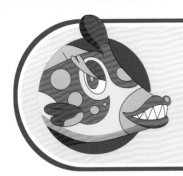

Bruxish
Slush

Bruxish scales have beautiful patterns, but it's best to observe them from a safe distance, as their sharp, grinding teeth are dangerous. This slush has its own beautiful pattern and the flavour has a bite to it!

Difficulty: ● ○ ○ ○
Prep Time: 30 minutes
Rest Time: 8 hours
Yield: 3 drinks

Equipment: 2 ice cube trays, blender

Blue Ice Cubes
7 butterfly pea flowers
1 tablespoon green tea
1 cup (240 millilitres) hot water

Pink Ice Cubes
¼ cup (60 grams) frozen raspberries
1 cup (240 millilitres) hot water
1 drop pink food colouring (optional)

Per Serving
4 blue ice cubes
3 pink ice cubes
1 cup (240 millilitres) lemonade

note: You can use shop-bought or Ampharos's Lemonade (page 33).

To make the blue ice cubes:
1. Place the butterfly pea flowers and green tea in a cup with a sieve. Add the water and let brew for 5 minutes.

2. Strain and transfer to an ice cube tray and allow to cool. Place in the freezer for at least 8 hours before using.

To make the pink ice cubes:
1. Place the raspberries in a cup with a sieve. Add the water and let brew for 5 minutes. Add the pink food colouring.

2. Strain and transfer to an ice cube tray and allow to cool. Place in the freezer for at least 8 hours before using.

For assembly:
1. Take the blue ice cubes and place them in the blender. Blend until the ice is crushed. Transfer to a cup.

2. Clean out the blender. Place the pink ice cubes in the blender and blend until the ice is crushed. Place in the same cup with the crushed blue ice.

3. Pour the lemonade into the cup and enjoy.

Alolan Exeggutor
Tall Tropical Slushie

Did you know that blazing sunlight has brought out the true form and powers of this Pokémon? I bet we can make an equally powerful drink by combining three delicious tropical fruits!

Difficulty: ● ○ ○ ○
Prep Time: 15 minutes
Yield: 1 Alola-size serving or 2 Kanto-size servings

Equipment: Blender

9 ounces (255 grams) frozen mango chunks
12 ounces (340 grams) frozen pineapple chunks
4 ounces (110 grams) ice
1½ cups (360 millilitres) coconut water

Place all the ingredients in a blender and blend until smooth. If making an Alola-size serving, serve in one large cup. If making a Kanto-size serving, split between two glasses.

Galar Region

Eldegoss
Toxtricity
Centiskorch
Clobbopus
Morpeko
Cufant

Eldegoss
Spinach Mushroom Burger

Eldegoss loves to spread its seeds to the wind to help benefit other Pokémon. You could do the same if you shared these delicious mushroom burgers with friends. Although they are so delicious that you might not want to share!

Difficulty: ● ● ○ ○
Prep Time: 30 minutes
Rest Time: 2 hours
Cook Time: 30 minutes
Yield: 6 burgers

Equipment: Large bowl, rolling pin, baking paper, large saucepan with steamer basket, stand mixer with dough hook attachment, large baking sheet

Steamed Buns

1 tablespoon active dry yeast
¾ cup (180 millilitres) warm water, plus more for steaming

> **note:** It is very important that the water is no warmer than 110°F (40°C) because if it is any warmer, it will kill the yeast and not allow the dough to rise. You can use a meat thermometer to check the temperature.

¼ cup (60 millilitres) rapeseed oil
2¾ cups (440 grams) plain flour
¼ cup (35 grams) cornflour
1 tablespoon baking powder
¼ cup (50 grams) sugar
2 teaspoons rock salt
Black sesame seeds for garnishing

Mushroom Burgers

1 shallot, chopped
4 garlic cloves, crushed
¼ cup (60 millilitres) balsamic vinegar
3 tablespoons olive oil
6 portobello mushrooms, stemmed

Per Serving

1 slice cheddar cheese (optional)
1 mushroom burger
1 steamed bun
Mayonnaise for topping
½ avocado, sliced
Cooked spinach for topping
Rocket for topping

To make the steamed buns:

1. Mix the yeast, water and rapeseed oil. Allow to rest for 5 minutes or until the yeast becomes active. Combine the flour, cornflour, baking powder, sugar and salt in the bowl of a stand mixer. Slowly mix in the liquid with the flour. Mix until it all comes together.

2. Transfer to a lightly floured surface and knead by hand for 5 minutes. Place the dough in an oiled bowl and cover. Let it rest until it doubles in size, about 2 hours.

3. Punch down the dough and roll out into a long tube. Split into six equal pieces and form into balls. Place each ball onto a sheet of baking paper and place in a steamer basket. Cover and allow to rest for 30 minutes. Lightly wet the tops of each of the rounds and place a few black sesame seeds on.

> **note:** Press lightly on the sesame seeds so that they stick without the pressure deflating the buns.

4. Heat a saucepan that the steamer basket can sit on with water over a high heat and bring to the boil. Once boiling, reduce the heat to medium and place the steamer basket with buns on top. Allow to steam for 15 to 20 minutes, until cooked through.

5. Turn off the heat and let sit, covered, for 5 minutes before using the buns. This will help prevent them from shrinking.

To make the mushroom burgers:

1. Combine the shallots, garlic, balsamic vinegar and olive oil. Place the mushrooms, top side down, on a foil-covered large baking sheet. Cover the inside of the mushroom with the dressing and allow it to marinade for at least 30 minutes.

2. Preheat oven to 375°F (190°C). Place the mushrooms in the oven and cook for 25 minutes, until the mushrooms are soft and cooked through.

For assembly:

1. If adding a slice of cheddar cheese to your serving, place on top of the cooked mushroom and place under the grill until it has melted, about 2 minutes.

2. Cut a bun open and cover the bottom half with mayonnaise. Top that with avocado slices and then the mushroom. Finally, top with spinach, rocket and the bun top.

Toxtricity
Blue & Yellow Smoothie

When Toxtricity generates a tremendous amount of electricity, it makes a sound that can resemble a daunting bass guitar. It's best to keep your distance, so enjoy a smoothie that matches your own mood!

Difficulty: ● ○ ○ ○
Prep Time: 20 minutes
Yield: 2 smoothies

Equipment: Blender

Purple Layer
1 banana
1 lime, juiced
¾ cup (180 millilitres) coconut milk
1 cup (160 grams) frozen pineapple chunks
½ cup (70 grams) frozen blueberries
½ cup (70 grams) frozen blackberries

Yellow Layer
½ banana
1 lemon, zested and juiced
1 lime, zested and juiced
2 tablespoons coconut milk
½ cup (80 grams) frozen pineapple chunks

Blue Layer
½ banana
⅓ cup (80 millilitres) coconut milk
½ cup (80 grams) frozen pineapple chunks
¼ teaspoon blue spirulina

To make the purple layer:
1. Place the banana, lime juice and coconut milk in a blender. Blend until smooth.

2. Add the pineapple, blueberries and blackberries. Blend until smooth. If the mixture is too thick, add additional coconut milk.

3. Split the drink between two large cups leaving about a quarter of the cup empty. Cover the glasses and place in the freezer until you make the other layers.

To make the yellow layer:
1. Clean out the blender. Place the banana, lemon zest and juice, lime zest and juice, and coconut milk in the blender. Blend until smooth.

2. Add the pineapple. Blend until smooth.

3. Take one of the glasses with the purple layer and top with the yellow layer.

To make the blue layer:
1. Clean out the blender. Place the banana and coconut milk in the blender. Blend until smooth.

2. Add the pineapple and blue spirulina. Blend until smooth.

3. Take one of the glasses with the purple layer and top with the blue layer.

Centiskorch
Spicy Tropical Curry

This spicy tropical curry is full of beautiful colours and patterns to match Centiskorch, but be careful when frying the plantains. You would be careful around a Centiskorch, and you should be just as careful with hot oil in the kitchen.

Difficulty: ● ● ○ ○
Prep Time: 45 minutes
Cook Time: 1 hour
Yield: 4 to 6 servings

Equipment: Medium saucepan with lid, large baking sheet, medium saucepan, medium non-stick pan, large bowl, small bowl

Saffron Rice

1 pinch saffron threads
¼ cup (60 millilitres) boiling water
2 tablespoons coconut oil
½ onion, finely chopped
2 garlic cloves, crushed
1¾ cups (360 grams) basmati rice
2 teaspoons rock salt
3¾ cups (900 millilitres) vegetable stock

Curry

4 maris piper potatoes, cut into 2-inch pieces
2 carrots, cut into 2-inch pieces
4 baby portobello mushrooms, quartered
2 tablespoons olive oil
Rock salt
Pepper
2 teaspoons garam masala
2 teaspoons cardamom
1 teaspoon ground turmeric
1 teaspoon paprika
1 teaspoon ground coriander
1 teaspoon ground cumin
1½ teaspoons Kashmiri chilli powder
½ teaspoon ground cinnamon
2 tablespoons coconut oil
½ red onion, chopped
1 tablespoon garlic paste
1 tablespoon ginger paste
14 ounces (395 grams) crushed tomatoes
14 ounces (395 grams) tomato sauce
½ cup (120 millilitres) vegetable stock
2 tablespoons coconut sugar
2/3 cup (160 millilitres) coconut cream
3 plantains, very ripe
Peanut oil for frying

To make the saffron rice:

1. Place the saffron and boiling water in a cup and allow to steep for 5 minutes. Heat a medium saucepan with coconut oil over a medium heat. Melt the coconut oil and add the onions and cook until translucent, about 5 minutes. Add the garlic and cook for another 2 minutes.

2. Add the rice and cook until slightly toasted, about 3 minutes. Add the saffron water, salt and vegetable stock. Bring to the boil and then turn the heat to low. Cover and cook until the rice has cooked, about 20 minutes.

To make the curry:

1. Preheat the oven to 425°F (220°C). Bring a medium saucepan of water to the boil and add the potatoes and carrots. Cook for 8 minutes, or until slightly tender. Transfer the potatoes and carrots to a large bowl with the mushrooms and olive oil. Place the oiled vegetables on a large baking sheet and sprinkle with salt and pepper. Bake for 20 minutes, toss and bake for another 15 minutes, or until tender.

2. While the vegetables are roasting, combine the garam masala, cardamom, turmeric, paprika, coriander, cumin, chilli powder and cinnamon in a small bowl. Heat a medium saucepan with coconut oil over a medium-high heat. Add the red onion and cook until translucent, about 5 minutes. Add the garlic and ginger paste and cook until fragrant, about 2 minutes. Add the spice mixture and mix until well combined.

3. Add the crushed tomatoes, tomato sauce and vegetable stock. Mix well, making sure there are no clumps of spices left. Simmer for 15 minutes.

4. Add the coconut sugar and coconut cream. Taste and season with salt and pepper if needed. Add the roasted vegetables and lightly mix until combined.

5. Prepare the plantains by cutting them open and slicing into ½-inch (10-millimetre) thick pieces and lightly salt. Fill a medium non-stick pan with ½ inch (10-millimetres) of peanut oil and heat over a medium heat. Once heated, carefully add the plantains and cook each side until golden, about 2 to 3 minutes per side.

6. Transfer to a paper towel on a plate to drain off the excess oil. Don't leave them on the paper towel for too long or they can get stuck. Serve warm.

7. To make a serving, place a portion of saffron rice on the plate and top with the curry. Place the plantains on top.

Clobbopus
Vanilla Punch

Difficulty: ●○○○
Prep Time: 15 minutes
Yield: 1 serving

Clobbopus likes to punch its surroundings to explore, but you shouldn't do the same. You wouldn't want to break anything or hurt anyone! Better to enjoy your punch as a drink than to throw one.

Equipment: Ice-cream scoop

1 scoop mango sorbet
2 scoops vanilla ice cream
8 fresh blueberries
½ cup (120 millilitres) fizzy orange drink
⅓ cup (80 millilitres) ginger ale

Place one scoop of mango sorbet into a large glass. Top with two scoops of vanilla ice cream. Add the blueberries. Pour in the fizzy orange drink and ginger ale. Serve with a spoon and straw to enjoy.

Morpeko
Crêpes

These amazing lemon and berry crêpes look just like Morpeko's different colours! Did you know Morpeko gets into trouble when it's hungry? Be sure to eat your fill so you don't end up the same.

Difficulty: ● ● ● ○
Prep Time: 45 minutes
Rest Time: 1 hour
Cook Time: 30 minutes
Yield: 6 to 10 servings

Equipment: Medium saucepan, whisk, blender, sieve, medium frying pan

Berry Curd
3 ounces (85 grams) fresh blueberries
4 ounces (110 grams) fresh blackberries
3 egg yolks
½ cup (100 grams) sugar
½ lemon, juiced
1 pinch rock salt
2 ounces (55 grams) unsalted butter

Lemon Curd
3 egg yolks
½ cup (100 grams) sugar
1 lemon, zested
⅓ cup (80 millilitres) lemon juice
1 pinch rock salt
2 ounces (55 grams) unsalted butter

Light Brown Crêpe
½ cup (80 grams) plain flour
1 pinch ground cinnamon
½ cup plus 2 tablespoons (150 millilitres) milk
1 egg
1 ounce (30 grams) unsalted butter, melted and cooled
½ tablespoon honey
1 teaspoon vanilla extract
Non-stick cooking spray for greasing
Whipped cream for garnishing

Dark Chocolate Crêpe
1 cup (160 grams) plain flour
2 tablespoons dark cocoa powder
1¼ cups (300 millilitres) milk
2 eggs
2 ounces (55 grams) unsalted butter, melted and cooled
1 tablespoon honey
2 teaspoons vanilla extract

To make the berry curd:
1. Place the berries in a blender and blend until smooth. Pass through a sieve. You want to end up with ⅓ to ½ a cup of juice.

2. In a medium saucepan, whisk the egg yolks, sugar and berry juice until the sugar dissolves and smooths. Add the lemon juice and salt. Place over a low heat and whisk until it thickens, about 10 minutes.

3. Add the butter. Whisk until the butter is completely melted. Strain into an airtight container and allow to cool completely. Place in the refrigerator for at least 1 hour before serving. The curd can be refrigerated for up to 1 week.

To make the lemon curd:
1. In a medium saucepan, whisk the egg yolks, sugar and lemon zest until the sugar dissolves and smooths. Add the lemon juice and salt. Place over a low heat and whisk until it thickens, about 10 minutes.

2. Add the butter. Whisk until the butter is completely melted. Strain into an airtight container and allow to cool completely. Place in the refrigerator for at least 1 hour before serving. The curd can be refrigerated for up to 1 week.

To make the light brown crêpe and dark chocolate crêpe:
1. To make the light brown crêpe: Place all the ingredients in a blender, except for the non-stick cooking spray and whipped cream, and blend until smooth. Transfer the batter into an airtight container and let rest in the refrigerator for at least 1 hour.

2. To make the dark chocolate crêpe: Repeat step 1 with the chocolate crêpe ingredients.

3. Remove the crêpe batter from the refrigerator and give it a good mix. Begin heating a medium frying pan on medium heat. Spray the pan with non-stick cooking spray. Using a ladle, pour ¼ to ½ a cup of batter onto the heated pan. Make sure to spread the batter around the frying pan so that the crêpe is nice and thin.

4. Cook the crêpe on one side for 3 to 5 minutes, or until it begins to brown. Carefully flip the crêpe and allow it to brown on the other side. Repeat with the remaining batter. Serve with the curds and whipped cream.

note: If you prefer, lemon and berry curd can be purchased ready made as well.

Cufant
Thai Iced Tea Float

Cufant is super strong. It's able to carry over five tons! Fortunately, this delicious iced tea float doesn't weigh that much, so you'll be able to enjoy it without requiring a Cufant to lift it for you.

Difficulty: ● ● ○ ○
Prep Time: 30 minutes
Rest Time: 12 hours
Cook Time: 30 minutes
Yield: 6 to 8 drinks

Equipment: Large saucepan, large jug, large bowl, medium bowl, whisk, stand mixer with whisk attachment

Thai Black Tea
4½ cups (1 litre) water
1 tablespoon coconut sugar
5 green cardamom pods, crushed
3 star anise pods
3 cloves
1 cinnamon stick
4 bags Ceylon tea
1 tablespoon vanilla extract

Vanilla Cardamom Ice Cream
14 ounces (400 grams) sweetened
    condensed milk
1 vanilla pod, seeds scraped and pod discarded
½ teaspoon ground cardamom
1 tablespoon vanilla extract
1 pinch rock salt
2 cups (480 millilitres) double cream

Boba
5 cups (1200 millilitres) water
½ cup (90 grams) instant black tapioca pearls
2 tablespoons coconut sugar
2 tablespoons brown sugar

Per Serving
Boba for garnishing
3 scoops vanilla cardamom ice cream
1 cup (240 millilitres) Thai black tea
¼ cup (millilitres) coconut milk
Orange food colouring (optional)

To make the Thai black tea:

1. Combine the water, sugar, green cardamom pods, star anise, cloves and cinnamon stick in a large saucepan. Heat over a medium-high heat and bring to the boil. Reduce the heat and simmer for 15 minutes.

2. Remove from the heat, add the tea bags, cover and let steep for 10 to 15 minutes. Strain into a large jug and add the vanilla extract. Allow to cool completely and then place in the refrigerator to chill. The tea can be stored in the refrigerator for up to 2 weeks.

To make vanilla cardamom ice cream:

1. Combine the sweetened condensed milk, vanilla pod seeds, cardamom, vanilla extract and salt in a large bowl. Whisk together until well combined.

2. Place the double cream in the bowl of a stand mixer. Mix on a medium-high speed until the whipped cream forms medium peaks, about 2 minutes. Transfer to the bowl with everything else. Carefully fold in the whipped cream until it is well combined.

3. Transfer to an airtight container and spread into a smooth, even layer. Cover and place in the freezer for at least 5 hours before serving. This makes enough ice cream for six to eight floats.

To make boba:

1. Place a large saucepan with water over a medium-high heat. Bring to the boil and add the tapioca pearls. Stir and cook for 2 to 3 minutes, or until the pearls float.

2. Cover and reduce the heat to medium-low. Continue to cook for another 2 to 3 minutes.

3. Turn off the heat, keep covered and cook for another 2 to 4 minutes, or until the tapioca has softened completely.

4. Drain through a sieve and rinse thoroughly with cold water.

5. Combine the sugars and a ½ cup (120 millilitres) of hot water in a medium bowl. Whisk together until the sugar has dissolved. Add the tapioca and allow to rest for 10 minutes.

6. The boba can be stored in the refrigerator for up to 6 hours.

For assembly:

Prepare a glass by placing boba on the bottom. Add the ice cream. In another glass, combine the tea, coconut milk and food colouring. Mix together until combined. Pour into the glass with the ice cream and enjoy.

About the Author

Victoria Rosenthal launched her blog, Pixelated Provisions, in 2012 to combine her lifelong passions for video games and food by recreating consumables found in many of her favourite games. When she isn't experimenting in the kitchen and dreaming up new recipes, she spends time with her husband and corgi hiking, playing video games and enjoying the latest new restaurants. Victoria is also the author of *Fallout: The Vault Dweller's Official Cookbook*, *Destiny: The Official Cookbook*, *Street Fighter: The Official Street Food Cookbook* and *The Ultimate FINAL FANTASY XIV Cookbook*. Feel free to say hello on Twitter, Twitch or Instagram at PixelatedVicka.